Son of Prick:

Bullies Are Everywhere – Even at Home

by Xavier Joseph D'Marco

Diane C. D'Marco

DORRANCE PUBLISHING CO
EST. 1920
PITTSBURGH, PENNSYLVANIA 15238

Dorrance Publishing Co
585 Alpha Drive
Pittsburgh, PA 15238
Visit our website at *www.dorrancebookstore.com*

ISBN: 978-1-4809-8428-8
eISBN: 978-1-4809-8447-9

Son of Prick:

Bullies Are Everywhere – Even at Home

Forward

Bully
It's 8 AM, this hell I'm in
Seems I've crossed a line again
For being nothing more than who I am
So break my bones and throw your stones
We all know that life ain't fair
But there's more of us we're everywhere

We don't have to take this back against the wall
We don't have to take this, we can end it all

All you'll ever be is a fading memory of a bully
Make another joke while they hang another rope, so lonely
Push them to the dirt till the words don't hurt can you hear me
No one's gonna cry on the very day you die you're a bully

Think it through you can't undo
Whenever I see black and blue I feel the past, I share the bruise
With everyone who's come and gone
My head is clear my voice is strong, now I'm right here to right the wrong

We don't have to take this back against the wall
We don't have to take this we can end it all

All you'll ever be is a fading memory of a bully
Make another joke while they hang another rope so lonely
Push them to the dirt till the words don't hurt can you hear me
No one's gonna cry on the very day you die you're a bully

It's 8 AM, the hell I'm in
Your voice is strong, now right the wrong
All you'll ever be is a fading memory of a bully
Make another joke while they hang another rope so lonely
Push them to the dirt till the words don't hurt can you hear me
No one's gonna cry on the very day you die you're a bully

All you'll ever be is a fading memory of a bully
Make another joke while they hang another rope so lonely
Push them to the dirt till the words don't hurt can you hear me
No one's gonna cry on the very day you die you're a bully

We don't have to take this back against the wall
We don't have to take this we can end it all

I STARTED TO WRITE THIS BOOK IN JANUARY OF 2014. As I sat down at my desk, I turned on my Sonos Stereo System. The first song that played was a song by Shinedown called "Bully." I told my wife and we thought that it was ironic that of all of the songs that could have been playing on that day, this song was the first song that I heard. I didn't think much about this coincidence at the time, but now I believe that this was a message from God. I truly believe that this was his way of telling me that the path that I had chosen to get my story out was the best path.

The official video is remarkable and it really depicts people of all walks of life who have suffered at the hands of bullies. It also indicates that bullies come in all shapes and sizes. Conversely, victims and targets of bullies come in all shapes and sizes and many of them are helpless children. My sisters and I grew up as victims of our father who was a bully.

Your neighbor next door could be a bully. Your co-worker could be a great work buddy but he or she could be hiding the same kind of secret. The words to this song are so appropriate and do capture the ordeal that the victims of domestic abuse go through on a daily basis. This video is amazing and really sets the tone for this topic in a very true and artistic way.

XJD

Table of Contents

Xavier Joseph D'Marco
January 22, 2017

Patrick D'Marco

Dear Dad:

I reached out to you last month so that we could have an intelligent conversation about some things. I expressed my condolences about Joanne's passing. You took the opportunity to blast my wife and blame her for things that she did not deserve. Before I could respond, you abruptly hung up on me.

Life is full of choices. An example of this is when you spoke to Diane about four years ago in 2013. She tried to have a heart-to-heart conversation with you. She explained that we were having difficulties with our teenage daughter and since Marisa was working and going to school, it was hard to get our family together and come over to your home. We always invited you both to our home. In addition, Joanne never really showed any interest or affection for our children. This is because you both felt that we did not roll out the red carpet. Joanne certainly had grievances about several incidents that took place over the years. In the past, I tried to discuss them with you both but Joanne was never willing to move past them. She carried her grudges for years.

Diane was merely explaining that it was evident that spending time with us in any capacity was an effort for Joanne. That really pissed you off and you twisted that statement into a pretzel. Four years later, you told me that we did not like your wife. That was the under-lying reason why you walked away from us in 2013. Please note that your version of events is wrong. My kids felt that Joanne did not like them and actions speak louder than words. Kids are very perceptive and my kids are no different than other children.

Many years ago, you told us a story about a Christmas party that you attended. It was hosted by Joanne's employer. One of the workers came up to you and asked if you were Joanne's husband. When you replied that you were, he said that, "Joanne is such a bitch." I personally would not have repeated that story to anyone, but you did. No one would ever say that about my wife.

When my kids did not want to go to your home, they would say that Grandma Joanne hated them. When you combine my kid's feelings with the Christmas party story, it makes my wife's statement that, "Joanne was cold to my kids," a realistic possibility.

Last month, you told me that, "you did not like Joanne when she was alive, so you don't like her in death." Before I could respond, you hung up the phone. Please note that we never disliked Joanne. Joanne was part of the family for the past thirty years or so and we felt terrible when we learned the news. Our family is very dysfunctional and even you should be able to admit this.

Think about this - you have three kids and none of them speak with you. I have heard you blame my mother for this fact: "My ex-wife poisoned their minds." That statement sounds good in theory but keep in mind that I was eighteen years old when you divorced my mother. My sisters were a little younger but we were not youngsters at the time. There were never any custody issues.

When I think of all the excuses and ridiculous statements that you have thrown out there over the years, it makes me laugh. You use the *Book of Excuses* just like Hillary Clinton. It is always someone else's fault. Here are just a few for your perusal:

- "My ex-wife poisoned their minds,"
- "My mother ruined my first marriage and I won't let that happen again,"
- "I paid too much attention to my house instead of my marriage,"
- "I hit you twice in your life and you deserved it both times,"
- "Two against one, so where should I punch you?"
- "You should rap her in the mouth,"
- "When God told you to get in line for brains, you thought he said pains,"

- "My wife is more important to me than my kids" (stated in 2013),
- "My wife is not allergic to dogs but when you put three of them together, it is a different story,"
- "If Marisa is allergic to peanut butter, can she have peanuts?"

I always tell my wife and my kids that life is full of choices. Four years ago, you decided to walk away from me and my family. At the time, I said to my wife that, "my father will always be a lonely, bitter, old man." Let's set the record straight, I got in the line for brains. My sense of perception dwarfs most individuals and I can see through all of the bullshit.

I have enclosed some photos for you. I thought that you should know that life does go on and we are all moving forward with our lives. Here are some of the highlights:

- Donna got married two years ago and lives on Park Avenue in NYC with her husband (she doesn't want you to know that she got married). She is retired.
- Nicholas is a father to Ariana Marie, which makes you a great-grandfather. I guess congratulations are in order.
- Michael graduated from an automotive school in Ohio. BMW hired him for an internship because of his good grades.
- Sally has diabetes and other serious health problems.
- Joseph is currently attending Molloy College.
- Marisa graduated college and works for an insurance company in Rockville Centre. Despite all of our problems with her during her teenage years, she now is a lovely, beautiful young woman and we are very proud of her. Please note that I never did "rap her in the mouth."
- My heart situation is so severe, that I had to retire at the age of fifty-two. I have plenty of time on my hands and you and I could have spent time together.

You chose to live your life one way and I chose to live my life another way. Only God will judge us. A perfect example is that Diane and I handled our daughter our way instead of beating the shit out of her like you thought we should have done. Eventually, she came around. The most important thing is that she loves us and respects us. We did the best that we could with her and we have no regrets.

I know that you and Joanne had your grievances with us. I came over to your home two different times to discuss your issues. On one occasion, I did discuss your wife's issues. Despite this, she never could let it go. On the other occasion, I met with you to discuss your issues and you told me to forget about it and stated to me that "my issues are not a big deal." That was your last opportunity to discuss issues and you chose to pass on that opportunity. Obviously, you couldn't let it go. Look where we are now.

Let me explain some of my issues with you:

- You went on vacation weeks before my open-heart surgery. My surgery was a life-saving surgery and, due to excessive bleeding, I had to go back into the OR to find the source of the bleeding. My point here is that I nearly died and if the roles were reversed, I would have spent as much time with my son as possible before the surgery. Don't feel bad, Mom did the same thing.
- On March 14, 1997 I had my surgeries. You didn't even take the day off from work. Something happened on the job and people heard you on the pay phone trying to fix the problem. Then you ran out of the hospital and stated that Grandma fell but you were really working. You needed that time off to build your garage and could not waste a vacation day on your son who could have died on the operating table.
- Once I came home from the hospital (one week later), we never saw you again. That was because you were building your precious garage and could not be bothered.
- When you told Grandma that I had the heart surgery, she wanted

to come to see me. You were too busy with your garage. You called me to get your mother off your back. Since I was such a good son, I did as you asked. Perhaps a visit from my grandmother would have been a good thing for both me and her. Again, you were too busy to be bothered. I was very depressed during my six-month recovery and you and Mom were a big part of that.

- Between you and Mom, someone came up with a story about Diane not allowing you to come to my home to visit your son. **This is such bullshit since Diane never made such a statement.** That was your excuse to not take any time away from your garage. Perhaps your misplaced priorities may explain why you have three children and they don't have any contact with you. Like I said before - **Life is full of choices.**

- You told my wife that you bought my first car. Remember that blue Dodge Dart that cost $800? You looked over the car and told me to "pay the man." I did pay him with eight one hundred-dollar bills. That was money that I earned cutting lawns.

- When it was obvious that Joanne did not want to be bothered coming to our home, my wife suggested that you come to see your grandchildren by yourself. I thought that my wife made an excellent suggestion. Your reply was, "I will never leave my wife." That was the perfect solution for your problem. You had nothing but time on your hands as Joanne was still working. We always treated you well and you really enjoyed spending time with Marisa and Joseph.

- When I told you that my son had severe social anxiety and school refusal, you stated that you could have fixed the problem. Kicking him down the stairs and out the door would have been your solution, but of course Diane and I would not have allowed such barbaric practices. Instead, we chose a Harvard-educated psychiatrist and a very competent psychologist. Joseph spent years in therapy and we spent a small fortune on his mental health care. It worked and he is going to college and loving it. We did it our way and I would not change a thing. The most important thing to me is that my son loves and respects me.

- You were always putting people down. Every time that you saw me, you would pat my stomach to let me know that you could see my belly. Then you would tell me to work out and lose it. Thanks Captain Obvious.

- You always reminded Sally that she was overweight. One day I told you to leave her alone and reminded you that she had mirrors in her home. Was your purpose to put her down or tell her something that she hadn't noticed?

- When I was seven years old and got my first pair of glasses, I was very embarrassed to wear them. Perhaps you were trying to build up my confidence when you said "look at your brother, he has four eyes."

- I always had a decent relationship with my three first cousins. You took the opportunity to ruin those relationships with your stories and exaggerations. Now I don't have a relationship with any of them. All I can say is good job. What you did here is sell your falsehoods to people who believed you. Like a car salesman, you sealed the deal.

- Aunt Anne Marie told me recently that "your father loves you." I was polite to her but when I got off the phone, I told my wife that those were just words. I believe that actions speak louder than words and I have had a lifetime of stories and comments made by you that dispute her assertion.

If you ever want to talk to me, call my cell number. Perhaps we can have a reasonable and informative conversation.

Sincerely,
Xavier J. D'Marco

Dedication

Son of Prick: Bullies are Everywhere - Even at Home is dedicated to the sixth-grade student who got off at my bus stop to protect me from a bully many years ago. She stood up to one of her classmates who had been bullying me when I was a first grader. I wish more people had the courage that she displayed on that particular day. In addition, I also wish that I had thanked her for her efforts to protect a younger and weaker child from a bully and predator.

Acknowledgments

This creative work of art would not have been possible without the love and support of my wife and children. They were very supportive when I discussed this project with them. The only caveat that they expressed was that they worried about my mental health when reviewing and writing about things that have occurred in my lifetime. Once I assured them that I would not live in the past, they agreed that this would be a good thing to do. Their support never wavered and this book has propelled me into the future. My past is my past and it remains in my rear-view mirror as we go forward in life.

God has been good to us and also contributed in his own way. I am grateful for his assistance in allowing me to produce one of the signature achievements in my life.

XJD

Introduction

Bullying is an awful act that belittles a person or a group of people and makes them feel inadequate. It can destroy a person's self-esteem. The dictionary indicates that a bully is, "a person who hurts, frightens, or tyrannizes over those who are smaller or weaker." This makes sense but sometimes the people being bullied are actually bigger than the bullies themselves. In my lifetime, I have been bullied and have watched others suffer at the hands of bullies. I have seen the results of bullying firsthand and I have seen other people being crushed by this despicable act.

My story is no different than perhaps someone who lived one hundred years ago. Bullying has been around since the beginning of time. Bullies enjoy picking on a person and making them feel inferior. Sometimes, bullies need a group of people around so that they can show off. The bigger the audience, the bigger the high that they get.

My maternal grandmother was born to immigrant parents and lived with them in Harlem in the 1920's. They only spoke Italian in the apartment so when Frances went to school, she had to learn English. The kids in her classes bullied her and called her the "Little Guinea." She learned from her experiences and lived her life to the fullest. When you spoke with her, you could never detect even a hint of an accent. She never spoke freely about being bullied, but she did tell me stories about these experiences when I asked.

When I was in the first grade, I was bullied by a sixth grader. Every day this bully and I would get off the school bus at the same bus stop. He would hit me and send me home bleeding every day. I would get cleaned up when I went home and didn't tell my parents that this was going on. This went on day after day until a sixth grader told him to pick on someone his own size. Bless her heart, she was able to stop something that went on for months in a matter of minutes. She stood between me and the bully and prevented him from even getting near me. He grumbled a bit but didn't have anything to say. She asked him why he was picking on me and he didn't have an answer for her. He turned around and walked away. He never bothered me again. I never even thanked that courageous girl but she was very compassionate. If I were to meet her today, I would certainly thank her for getting involved and helping out a little kid who needed help.

My experience with that sixth-grade bully is probably the common type of bullying story that you would normally hear about. The bully in that situation was someone who I didn't know, but for whatever reason decided that he didn't like me. It could have been my appearance that he didn't like or the clothes that I wore. We had similar backgrounds as we both lived in a middle-class neighborhood in Queens, New York. He was twelve years old and graduating our elementary school at the end of that school year. I was eight years old and still getting used to the neighborhood that we had recently moved to. I know that I never did anything to offend him or make him dislike me. He bullied me because he knew that he could get away with it.

I decided to write this book because bullying is a horrible thing that can affect someone for the rest of their lives. I was bullied by my father for the first eighteen years of my life. I don't know what I ever did to this man but his actions indicate a deep-seated hatred for me, for whatever reason. I was subjected to his wrath for a very long time. It couldn't have been my appearance because I looked like him and my mother. It couldn't have been my actions because I did everything that he asked of me. I didn't complain about the way he treated me and I was very compliant. I did all of my chores and stood right next to him for every second that he needed help when he worked around the house. I often wondered if he treated me this way because, as a child, I was always sick and needing medical attention. Perhaps he was jealous because my mother had to focus a lot of attention on me due to my medical issues. This would have been time that she would have normally focused on her husband. Perhaps, I was not the son that he felt that he deserved.

Pat claims that the day that I was born was the happiest day of his life. I didn't believe him when he said those words because I knew how I was treated. I wouldn't have treated a dog the way that he treated me. We have a dog living in our home who I am not fond of. Every chance that this dog gets, he lifts his leg and squirts. That is his "F.U." to me. He leaves urine in my kitchen and my entire backyard is his toilet. He is one of three little dogs that we own, but I don't treat him badly. I only yell at him when I catch him pissing in my kitchen. I don't hit him or hurt him in any way. When I yell, I certainly get his attention. His name is Angel and he definitely is not an angel. The funny thing is that he lives in a wonderful, safe home that is certainly better than where he could have wound up if my wife and I hadn't decided to take him in. My mother-in-law was going to try to find a home for him and my father-in-law asked us to take him in. Our kids also appreciated that we saved Angel from an uncertain future.

A parent is someone who is supposed to protect their children. I know because my wife and I have two children. They were helpless and totally dependent on us as infants. They would not have survived if we did not feed them, love them, and provide shelter for them. We protected them from all of life's hazards to the best of our abilities. We were always there for them. Now we have two well-adjusted grown children and this is a testament to our loving guidance and nurturing and they both appreciate the parents that we have become. Diane and I provided a wonderful and loving home in a nice neighborhood and they feel the safest when they are in the confines of our home.

My father did not protect me. Instead, he used me as his whipping boy. When things didn't go well, he hit me over and over again. He did not provide a loving home that I felt safe in. He provided a cold building with four walls that I hated to be in. The neighborhood was beautiful and above his means but all he cared about was living in Whitestone, Queens. The problem was that he didn't care enough about the people living in this house and, in the end, he found himself all alone.

I am writing this book to provide an eye-witness account of bullying in general. In order to do this, I must expose my father for the animal that he is and always was. Pat has taught me a lot over the years but it wasn't intentional. I learned how to be a good father by **not** using him as an example. He didn't try to teach me to be a good father. I just knew enough to **not** be a father like he was. When your children do something wrong, you don't need to beat them to teach them. You try talking to them and punish them with a reasonable punishment. It certainly doesn't hurt to find out what led to that moment so that this situation can be corrected. I was caught cutting school when I was fifteen years old. My father beat the crap out of me and kicked me down two flights of stairs. Did I learn from his punishment? No. Instead, I ramped it up and was determined to not get caught next time.

My father truly believes that he was a good father. He told me that he was, "a good father because none of my kids got arrested or got knocked up." If my sisters or I would have gotten arrested, he would have been the last person that we would have called. If either of my two sisters had gotten pregnant, then perhaps they might have had an abortion to solve the problem. He would never have known. If you ask me, his benchmark is set really low.

Communicating with your children is very important. I try to share my experiences with my children to teach them. When they have a problem, my wife and I sit down with our kids to help them to resolve their problems or situations. My father never tried to explain to me why I did something wrong. He started swinging and asked questions after the fact. Pat never provided one ounce of parental guidance to me. I probably wouldn't have had much faith in his solutions if he had provided any advice. I asked his opinion once when I was a teenager. The situation involved a friend of mine and when he heard the facts, he assumed that I was the person needing the advice. He started yelling at me and I swore that I had nothing to do with the scenario. That incident was certainly a learning moment for me. Unlike my old man, I was smart enough to avoid making that mistake again.

I tell my kids that there aren't any problems that we can't fix. We just need to sit down and discuss the issue and try to find reasonable solutions. I actually feel very good when our kids do come to us looking for advice and we can help them to craft solutions.

This book is about my experiences as a victim of bullying from a person whom I trusted and who was supposed to protect and guide me into adulthood. My children also experienced bullying in grade school and I wanted to touch upon their experiences as well. I witnessed a classmate being bullied in junior high school and witnessed several colleagues at work who were bullied. I didn't try to help my classmate and I regret that decision, but I was trying to fit into a new school and was trying to learn how to function as a thirteen-year old teenager. In addition, I did not want to be targeted as this person was. Perhaps, this book will enable someone to stand up on behalf of a person being bullied like the sixth-grade girl who helped me out in 1970.

Humble Beginnings

My name is Xavier Joseph D'Marco and I was born in 1962 in the Bronx, New York. My family and friends call me Joe for short. I have heard many people state that "they broke the mold" after so and so was born. In my case, they just changed the name of the hospital. Misericordia Medical Center on 233rd Street merged with Our Lady of Mercy Medical Center after I was born. It is now known as the Wakefield Campus of Montefiore Medical Center. I have been to this hospital in my adult life and it is a very busy hospital in a very busy section of New York City.

In the old days, expecting fathers would not be in the birthing rooms when their children were born. They would wait in the waiting room and they would see their child or children afterwards. My father, Pat, showed up with cigars after I was born. He worked for the local electric company for the five boroughs of New York City. The three of us lived in an apartment in the Bronx for two years and then moved in with my paternal grandmother Nancy, who owned a house in Queens. As the family continued to grow, we eventually moved to our own house which was located in the Rosedale section of Queens. I lived with my two sisters (Sally and Donna), my Grandma Nancy, and my two parents Pat and Marie. This house was sold when I was five years old and we eventually moved to Whitestone, Queens when I was seven years old.

My story begins in the Rosedale home. We lived in a two-story house which had an apartment on the second floor. An older couple lived in that apartment and rented it from my father. We lived on the first floor in a small area that was comprised of two bedrooms, a kitchen, full bath, living room, and dining room. These were tight quarters for six people to be living in together.

There was a supermarket across the street. I learned how to ride a bicycle in the parking lot of this store. I crashed into a girl who was also learning how to ride her bicycle on that same day. My mother, Marie, worked part time at this store as a bookkeeper. Grandma Nancy would return home from work and take me to the supermarket and buy me all of the candy that I wanted. To this day, I have a sweet tooth. My parents would argue with my grandmother because I wouldn't eat my dinner after I feasted on chocolate. I was the first of her six grandchildren and she loved spoiling me.

I attended the public school which was located near our home. I walked to and from school by myself to go to kindergarten. 228th Street was an extremely busy street and I was not allowed to cross this street by myself. I recall that there was a plane crash near our neighborhood during the school year. We were living in an area that was right near John F. Kennedy International Airport. I was in class one day and we were watching the helicopters scour the area searching for wreckage. Other than that incident, my kindergarten year at this school was uneventful.

I was friendly with a young boy who was in my class. Terrance lived one block from my home on the other side of 228th Street. One day after school, I went to his home and we played for the entire afternoon. Terrance's father was a doctor and he was home and talking with us as we played in his basement. We then went outside to play in the backyard. They had a stockade fence in their yard that kept us safely in the backyard. My young friend and I were climbing the fence and walking along the horizontal cross members of the fence. My father happened to come by to bring me home for dinner and saw us on the fence. I recall waving to my father as I stood on the crossmember of the fence when he came to pick me up. We were just being boys and horsing around. We didn't damage anything and the owner of the home didn't reprimand us for walking along the fence. As soon as my father and I left the home, Pat hit me repeatedly in the front of this home. This may not seem like an important point but it is significant because this is my earliest recollection of being viciously punched and kicked by my father. I was just a cute little kid who wouldn't hurt a fly. I was now being subjected to beatings that were, at times, brutal. It was at this moment in time that I began to fear this man.

I cannot psychoanalyze Pat to understand why a man in his twenties would hit a five-year old boy repeatedly for doing something that he perceived as being wrong. At the age of five, I did not understand that my father had mental issues that were never addressed and his actions were unacceptable. I grew up fearing this man and he knew that and he thrived on it. He once told me that he and I were going to fight it out one day and he was "going to kick the shit" out of me. I was still in elementary school when he made that statement. What do you say to a man who thinks that this is an appropriate statement to make to a child? I often wondered if this was his goal in life, to beat his offspring. If it was, mission accomplished.

I cannot justify my father's behavior in any way, shape, or form. He had a difficult childhood in a tough neighborhood in the Bronx. Does that mean that my childhood should have been difficult also? His father was a boxer who used to hit his two boys. I never met Grandpa Joe but I heard that he was tough on his boys. My grandfather died of a heart attack before I was born. He and Grandma Nancy had a tough job raising two boys in the Arthur Avenue section of the Bronx and working to support their family. Grandpa Joe's kids were mischievous, but again, they were just being boys. My grandfather's solution to dealing with sons (who were always fighting with one another) was to hit his kids when they were out of line. Then he forced them to enlist into the military after they graduated from high school.

When I went to the doctor for checkups as a young boy, the doctors would all listen to my heart attentively because I had a heart defect. This defect was called a heart murmur which meant that some blood was leaking backwards into the previous heart chamber instead of moving forward and into the next chamber. The doctors would let me listen to my defect by using their stethoscopes. They would also allow me listen to their hearts so that I could hear the differences in both of our hearts. When I was five years old, I contracted a disease called rheumatic fever which is caused by strep throat.

The treatment involved taking antibiotics until the infection was eradicated. I remember that every Friday, my mother and I would get on a bus and take it to the hospital. The nurses would slice one of my fingers open with a razor blade and squeeze blood onto a glass slide. This seems quite barbaric but that is how it was done in the 1960s. The band-aid was quite boring and not as colorful and cheerful as the band-aids that today's children enjoy. The process was painful and the next week we would repeat the entire process over again. My blood would be examined under a microscope to see if the infection was still active. This went on for months and I would give my mother a hard time about going to the hospital.

I was a sickly child because of the rheumatic fever and heart condition. I had to be careful when I went to the dentist due to this heart problem. The dentist would give me antibiotics at the time of my dental visit and I would have to take the rest of the pills after my visit. As I got older, my mother stopped monitoring me following the dental visits and I would just take the antibiotics (four large pills) that the dentist gave to me before he cleaned my teeth. The antibiotics that I was supposed to take for seven to ten days following the visit just went into my underwear drawer. I would periodically clean out my drawer and throw away all of the pills that I was supposed to have taken. That underwear drawer had dozens of bottles in it. The ironic thing about my life is that when I was twenty-six years old I took every last pill that I was supposed to take following a dental visit and yet I contracted a serious and life-threatening heart infection.

I don't know how my father felt about having a sick child. I never asked him. It never stopped him from putting me to work or beating me for whatever crimes that I had committed. He was never sick in his entire life and I guess that he felt I should have been stronger than I was. Perhaps I was not the type of son that he could be proud of. He certainly treated me like he hated me from early on.

Except for the heart issues, I had contracted the same illnesses that most children get. I had the chicken pox, measles, mumps, and knee issues that affected both knees. When I was in school, we had health insurance that New York City provided because my mother worked for the New York City Housing Authority. The insurance was adequate and my parents certainly got their money's worth out of this plan. I was always going to the Hip Center in Flushing for medical visits.

While we were living in Rosedale, there was an incident that occurred when I was coming home from kindergarten. I was walking home from school with another boy and I was not allowed to cross 228th Street. Every day, I would wait at the corner of the intersection at 228th Street for someone to accompany me across the street. One sunny afternoon, our neighbor, Gladys, was supposed to meet me at the corner and watch me for the afternoon. She had five children of her own but she was helping out my mother that day. I was waiting on the corner and sitting on a brick wall. I had my bank book with me which had my name and address in it. At the time, we would bring our bank books to school and the school would deduct the cost of our mid-morning snack and milk. This amounted to pennies every week. I left the bank book on the brick wall. The boy that I was with dared me to pull the fire alarm box that was on the corner. It was a tall red metal unit with a handle. If someone pulled the handle, it would alert the fire department that there was a fire in the neighborhood. I was tall enough to reach the handle and we wanted to see what would happen. I pulled the lever and the fire alarm worked perfectly! Alarms started going off when I pulled that handle. My partner-in-crime and I ran as fast as our little legs could carry us. My friend disappeared and I ran up the block, turned around, and started walking back to the corner as if I didn't have a care in the world. I was panicking inside because I knew that I had done something wrong. I reached the corner and Gladys met me there and took me across the street and into her home for a peanut butter sandwich. She had no idea that I pulled that lever.

The fire department arrived at the scene and determined that this was a false alarm. One of the firemen found my bank book and felt that a house call was in order. Later that night, the doorbell rang. The fire inspector was returning my bank book and had some questions for me. He explained that false alarms can cause people to get hurt. If the fire department is called to a false alarm, they may not be available for a real fire. In addition, a fireman was killed weeks earlier when he fell off a truck responding to another false alarm. The fire inspector asked me if I pulled the lever on the fire alarm box. I responded that I did and I apologized for doing such a stupid thing. He told me that if I did that again, I would really be in trouble. I assured him that I would never do that again.

I handled the situation well but fear started to set in because I knew that my father was coming home and I didn't want to get another beating. I feared my father and what he would do when he learned about my reckless act. To my surprise, he spoke to me in a stern voice and did not hit me. I promised him that I would never touch that fire alarm box again.

I recently discussed this incident with my mother and she told me that Pat thought that what I did was funny. I reminded him of himself when he was a kid. Of course, he couldn't tell that to me. My "Oh Shit" moment turned out to be a funny story that he could tell the guys at work. It wouldn't be the last stupid thing that I did in my life.

Weeks later, me and several friends climbed a tree and entered a house on my block that had been destroyed by a fire. The fact that this house was condemned did not deter several curious boys. We climbed onto the second floor and were then stuck there since we could not get down. Pat came home from work and rescued all of us using his ladder.

The D'Marco family moved to 14th Avenue in Whitestone Queens in 1969. Grandma Nancy no longer lived with us as she owned a house in Woodhaven, Queens. The home that my parents purchased was an old home that needed new electric, insulation in the walls, new doors and windows, new plumbing, etc. My father's intention was to gut the house, room by room, and redo the entire house. He planned to put his son to work since I was free labor. When my classmate Jay Berger would call me because they were getting a football game together, I would ask my father if I could go to play with my friends. Pat would usually tell me that he needed me and I would have to decline the invitation. It didn't matter that it was the weekend and I wanted to play with my friends. I declined more football, basketball, and baseball games than I could count over the years. I told my father years later that he stole my childhood from me. His response was that he needed the help.

Look Who Is Calling the Kettle Black

My family moved to a house located in Whitestone, Queens in 1969. I was seven years old and starting a new school in the first grade. The school was P.S. 193. My seat was in the rear of the classroom due to my height and my grades were not very good. Then the public schools started mandatory eye testing for all of the students in the entire school and it turned out that I needed glasses at the age of seven. My sight was really bad but no one bothered to check until I was in the first grade. Once I started seeing the world using glasses, my grades improved dramatically. My mother then met with the principal and insisted that I be moved into a class that reflected my test grades. The class that I was transferred into was in the IGC Program which meant *Intellectually Gifted Children*. I excelled in this program and remained with my classmates until graduation at the end of the sixth grade. Jay Berger was one of my classmates and we remain friends to this day.

Every school in New York City required teachers and parents to get together at least one time per year to discuss the student's progress. Today, that trend continues. Parents get dragged down to parent-teacher conferences each and every year. My parents would go to the conferences and the teachers would rave about how intelligent I was and how well I was doing in school.

The truth of the matter is that I never had to study for exams. I would attend classes and retain the information so well that I aced all of my exams. Jay

Berger would go home to prepare for an exam and I would go out and play basketball or baseball. He would say to me, "What did you get on the math exam?" I would reply with my grade and he would say to me that, "You played basketball and didn't even study!" This pattern served me well throughout my early years but eventually it hurt me.

I attended the Bronx High School of Science in 1976. This school continues to be ranked in the top 100 schools in the entire country. They have the highest percentage of students attending college at nearly one hundred percent. I did well enough on the entrance exam to be accepted to this remarkable school. My father was really proud of me being accepted to this school. He took my acceptance letter and I never saw it again. I assume that he used it to brag to his co-workers about how smart his son was.

I graduated from the Bronx High School of Science in 1980 with an eighty-four average. I never opened a book to study but did all of my work. The teachers in the school told us that whatever your grade point average was, you could add ten points and that is what you would have earned in any other school in the country. I believed the hype and continued my pattern of not studying. I could have and should have done better in school. I eventually found out that the teachers were wrong because I didn't get accepted to Fordham University which was the school that I really wanted to go to. I was accepted to Fairleigh Dickinson University in New Jersey for the Pre-Dental Program. My father was not willing to help me pay for this school so I had to reject the offer. I was deeply hurt by not being able to go to this school and be in a program that truly interested me.

In the fall of 1980, I began attending St. John's University in the pharmacy program. I was really enjoying college, perhaps too much. The transition from high school to college is difficult enough but when you combine the lack of studying with what was going on in my personal life, college for me became very difficult. In my second year of college I began swimming for the St. John's swim team. I was unable to swim in my freshman year because of a medical condition known as mononucleosis. The training was grueling and tiring and it made college even more difficult for me. My grades were even worse in the first semester of sophomore year and as a result I had to withdraw from the pharmacy program. I switched into the political science program. It was at this point that I had to quit the swim team and get my act together. I taught myself how to study and my grades improved quickly. In my junior and senior years, I did so well that I was making the dean's list each semester.

I went back to college in 2002 to obtain my second college degree. I enrolled in the accounting program of Molloy College in Rockville Centre. I was very unhappy working for the insurance company that I worked for. There was no upward mobility and their intent always seemed to be to pull out of the automobile insurance market in New York. I saw the writing on the wall and I was going to do something about it. In 2008, I graduated with a Bachelor of Science degree in Accounting. My 3.77 index qualified me as Magna Cum Laude in a very difficult program. I was able to balance a home life, work life, and night school for six years. What helped me through this process was the fact that I knew how to study and had the desire to succeed and this allowed me to excel in this program. My instincts were eventually proven correct because many of my co-workers and I were eventually laid off from the insurance company. I then used my accounting degree to get a government job as an auditor.

This background information is important and illustrates how I was able to breeze through school. I was accomplished in my school life as well as my work life. The reason that I even mention these things is because I had a father who constantly belittled me and made me feel bad about myself. If I earned a ninety-five on a test, he would ask why I didn't get a one hundred. Instead of praising me, he told me that I should have done better. When I look back, I realize that his shortcomings in life made him a miserable person and it made him feel better to constantly pounce on me and my feelings. He really excelled at putting people down and he took great pleasure in attacking me constantly.

Pat D'Marco, by comparison, has a very limited school background. He graduated from Samuel Gompers High School in the Bronx. It was a trade school and he learned automotive skills. That was the extent of his schooling. After high school, he went to work in a gas station. After two years in the navy, he returned home and began working for the electric company. When you talk to him, it is evident that he is not an educated man.

I started wearing glasses at the age of seven. Pat would call me "four-eyes" and he and my sisters would laugh about the fact that I needed to wear glasses in order to see. I wouldn't wear the glasses at home so that Pat could ridicule me. When I played basketball in the Catholic Youth Organization (CYO), I would not wear my glasses. If I missed a basket during a game, Pat would ridicule me for not scoring. Whether he made fun of me at the dinner table or in the car following a basketball game, it would make me feel horrible and hate this man.

Pat D'Marco needed my help on whatever project he was working on. I wouldn't wear my glasses because I didn't want to be a target of his jokes. Then, when he demanded that I pass a tool to him or grab something for him, I couldn't see what he was referring to. Pat would quickly lose his patience and then the personal insults were hurled at me. He would call me stupid in his very unsophisticated way. Most of the time, he would not be clear about what he wanted because he was not very good at communicating. He would call me names and repeat the same insults to me over and over again. He sounded like a broken record. Pat would say that "When God told everyone to get in line for brains, you didn't get on line because you thought that God said pains." This comes from a man who was called "anal" and he didn't know what the person meant until I enlightened him. This from a man who told people that his son was "lackadaisy" when he meant to say "lackadaisical" but the meaning of the word and the word itself escaped him. This, from a man who told people that he had "tree" kids instead of "three" kids. This from a man who told us that the allergy doctor that tested his second wife, Joanne, said that she was not allergic to dogs but when you put her in a room with three dogs, "it is a different story." This from a man who knew that my daughter, Marisa, had a serious allergic reaction to peanut butter but still asked if she could have peanuts. My father is truly an ignoramus but God bless him, he found someone to be his second wife and her IQ was also in the negative number range. Look who is calling the kettle black.

Meat but No Potatoes

Living under Pat's roof was not an ideal situation for any of us. It wasn't like living under a big beautiful rainbow and there certainly wasn't a yellow brick road that I could see. Pat always provided the meat but not the potatoes. Of course, the basics that he provided were always subjected to his interpretation and that could change at any time. Grandma Nancy saw this flaw in her son and that is why she would come to our neighborhood each month and shop at the local supermarket. She would buy the extras that Pat never provided. These items included soda, ice cream, cake, cookies, and, most importantly, chocolate. She would drop them off at our home and get on two buses to go back to her apartment.

We have a friend who comes to visit with my wife and I frequently. One of her kids loves the sweets and other goodies that we have stashed in our home. This one adorable child always knows what those goodies are and is not shy in asking for them. Sometimes when this little girl goes home, she is bouncing off the walls from all of the sugar. She does not get these items at home and tries to make up for it when she comes to our home. As a child, I was like that. I drank milk by the gallon and enjoyed juice as well. When someone offered me soda at their home, I would certainly get my fill.

Grandma Nancy would love to take me and my cousins to the movies. She loved us and loved spoiling us. My cousin Danny and I spent a weekend with her when we were in elementary school. She always planned fun things for us to do. The local movie theatre had an all-day screening of the *Planet of the Apes* movies. Danny and I loved those old movies. The three of us walked to the theatre and spent the entire afternoon watching those movies. We really had a good time. Grandma Nancy brought a big bag that had chocolate chip cookies, chocolate, and two bottles of root beer. What else could two seven-year old children want in life? Later that night, I puked all over the place and felt lousy but I would do it again in a heartbeat. Grandma Nancy is gone now and I really miss her. She was not a fan of the movies that we saw that day, but was willing to sit through them all day so that Danny and I could enjoy them. She enjoyed seeing us enjoy ourselves.

My grandmother must have seen things in her son that were disturbing. She lived into her nineties and was smart enough to see Pat's tendency to bully others. I suspect that he bullied her as well, but I have no proof. An old friend of our family claims that he saw Pat hitting Nancy when he stopped by Pat's home unexpectedly. This took place around 1996 when Nancy was in her late eighties. Several years later, she fell in his home and sustained a hemorrhage in her brain. She did recover physically from those injuries caused by the fall, but was never the same. She wound up in a nursing home and I would visit her weekly. She did not know who I was. I brought my wife and kids to see her in the home but she didn't recognize them either.

Living under Pat's roof was difficult for Nancy as she was totally reliant on her son. Pat would buy her groceries every week and one of those grocery items was dietetic bread. I tasted it once and it tasted like cardboard. Pat didn't let her have ice cream and other things due to her weight. What he didn't know is that an ice cream truck would stop in front of his house every day at 3:00 PM and Nancy would run out and buy goodies for herself! My sister, Sally, witnessed this and we laughed about it. Pat was at work and couldn't see what Nancy was doing when he wasn't home. Over the years, all of us tried to circumvent his control behind his back.

Grandma Nancy was your typical Italian grandmother. She stood about five feet tall and was a robust and jovial person. When she hugged me, she would squeeze me so tight. Her head only reached the middle of my chest. This woman lived her entire life as an overweight individual and Pat thought that he could make her lose weight in her eighties. I often wondered if he was preparing her for a swimsuit competition! Pat was only happy when he was mad at people and controlling others. His wife and kids bolted out of his home as soon as we could but Grandma Nancy had nowhere else to go. I realized her predicament and truly felt badly for her.

After I was married, my wife Diane, and I would periodically pick up Nancy so she could spend the weekend with us. We would let her enjoy her sweets and she would love the activity in our home. A typical weekend at our home consisted of Diane cooking lots of delectable Italian delights including spaghetti and meatballs. Grandma Nancy would love to eat real Italian bread and dip it in the gravy. Italians call it gravy, but it is technically a tomato sauce. My daughter would be running around the house and our dog Cookie would be running around as well. At night, we would eat pastries and gelato.

One night, Grandma Nancy was eating a dish of gelato that had hazelnuts in it. I noticed Marisa running past me with gelato on her face and since she is allergic to nuts, I was worried. I said to my grandmother "Did you give Marisa any of that gelato because she is highly allergic to nuts?" She replied that she hadn't given Marisa any, but the evidence was on my two-year old's face. Thankfully, Marisa did not have a reaction and we laugh about it as we fondly remember Grandma Nancy.

When I think back to those weekends that we entertained Grandma Nancy, we had a lot of fun with her. My in-laws loved her and enjoyed her company. Diane's grandmother, Lilly, would come over and hang out with Grandma Nancy also. The two old ladies would be chatting up a storm and enjoying each other's company in front of the fireplace in our home. Then they would argue about how you make a good meatball. Like I said earlier, Pat provided the meat, but not the potatoes.

Grandma Nancy was well-nourished but her subsistence was boring. I wouldn't feed my dogs dietetic bread but this lady could not physically get to a supermarket. When she came to our home, she enjoyed the food that we gave to her. She also enjoyed our company and spending time with her great-granddaughter. In a way, I did for Grandma Nancy what she did for us growing up. She would get her social security check and buy us goodies and then drop them off at our home. Now I reciprocated by bringing her into our world and she was enjoying the meat and the potatoes. I always took her to her doctor visits when I could, but allowing her to spend time with us was more valuable to her. The memories that we have will last a lifetime.

In my youth, I was in great shape. I joined the St. Luke's swim team when I was seven years old and I continued swimming into college. I was good, but certainly not an Olympian. One of the things that helped my physique was the constant work that Pat made me do. Pat's favorite picture of me is when I was seven years old and pushing a gas lawn mower for the first time. The photo was black and white and the handle bar was taller than I was. It is a nice photo of me in my youth, but it reminds me of the beginning of my work life for Pat.

The house that Pat and Marie bought in Whitestone was certainly a fixer-upper. Pat had a vision of what he wanted in his home. He didn't have the communication skills to make us understand what he was looking for. His plans were grandiose and very ambitious. There were times when he had his wife and three kids helping him with construction. I remember those times vividly and it consisted of him yelling at all of us and not being satisfied with what we were doing. Perhaps, he should have explained himself better. Instead, he yelled and humiliated us. Other times he used his tools and construction items as a weapon on me and my mother. I can understand that he might have been frustrated when we helped him, but he only made things worse when he called us stupid and ridiculed us. In the end, he always ended up with the results that he desired.

As a young boy, I was confused because when my mother accidentally fell down the stairs, my father ran over to help her. This type of reaction is what you would expect from a person who cared about his wife. Another time, I remember him hitting her in the back, neck, and head with a 2 x 4. This was a solid piece of wood that was roughly two inches by four inches in width. The piece that he used as a weapon was about four feet long and very solid. I ran to help my mother, but she told me to go back into my room. She was afraid that he would hit me with that same piece of wood. Years later, she told me that she had embarrassed Pat when she challenged something that he said in front of some friends. I asked him about this incident years later and, as expected, he denied that he ever hit my mother.

I have an allergy problem and I was always allergic to dust, grass, and pollen. If my father needed to get his money's worth out of me and didn't have work for me to do, he would invent new things for me to do. My favorite ridiculous job in retrospect was when his workroom needed a cleaning. He would give me a paint brush and make me dust the shelves. Then I would clean the workbench and sweep the floors. It would take me hours to complete this task. This would send my allergies into a frenzy and I would be sneezing and coughing the rest of the day. After his workroom was nice and clean, he would laugh at how miserable I looked and felt.

The workroom was in the basement and we had a table saw that Pat used to cut sheets of plywood and other things. A sheet of plywood is four feet wide and eight feet long. It is a bitch to cut because of its size and weight, but you need this kind of wood as a subfloor. We were cutting this plywood when we were redoing our kitchen. He was the captain and I was his co-pilot. I was supposed to hold the wood level and straight as he guided it into the table saw. The sawdust made me sneeze and as a result, the wood moved and was cut irregularly. Pat was a perfectionist and my actions were unacceptable so he kept yelling at me as I sneezed. Just for good measure, he punched me in the head when he got close enough to me. I knew that he was going to hit me because whenever something went wrong, I was his punching bag. The ironic thing about this wood was that no one would ever see it because a tile floor was to be installed on top of the plywood. I knew that and he knew that as well. That verbal and physical abuse was so unnecessary. All I can say is welcome to my world!

In looking back on this common occurrence, I realize that there was a very simple solution that could have avoided this problem. Had Pat spent a couple of bucks to buy disposable masks that covered my mouth and nose, his wood would have been cut perfectly. He knew that my allergies were a big problem for me. I would sneeze and then bleed profusely. Then we would go to the ER to get the blood vessels in my nose cauterized. Sometimes I would wake up in a pool of blood. Thankfully that is a thing of the past.

I was about nine years old when Pat and I gutted the kitchen. He did a beautiful job on that kitchen. When we ripped up the floor, the plywood had to be placed on the floor and then the ceramic tile went on top of the plywood. Plywood was expensive then and it still is. He found a lumberyard that had plywood on sale in Flushing. I was listening to the Jet game on this frigid Sunday as he and I travelled to the lumberyard several times that day. The roof of our car could only handle four boards at a time due to the weight of the plywood. He would tie the boards to the roof and I would have to hold the rope tight as we travelled with the windows open. During one of those trips, we were crossing a small bridge and a gust of wind blew the lumber off the roof. We stopped in the middle of the bridge and Pat went to retrieve one board at a time. He put the wood on the roof and made me hold the board in place as he went for the next board. I was standing on the rocker panel of the car and used my weight to hold the boards down until Pat came back. A gust of wind lifted one of the boards off the roof and I fell onto the pavement. This one sheet of plywood flew off the bridge. I was able to get up and look at the wood as it fell like a piece of paper. It floated downward until it landed in the river. An angel was on my shoulders that day because I could have landed in the water just like that plywood. I surprisingly didn't get in trouble for losing that one sheet of plywood. I heard him tell people about that incident and most people got a chuckle out of that story.

I honestly felt that Pat had mental issues due to his perfectionism. He would paint a wall even though it was going to be covered by cabinets. It was as if he was afraid that the *Cabinet Police* would criticize him for not having everything perfect. I was there every step of the way with the construction of the kitchen and adjoining laundry room. I was his helper with every job that he worked on, even jobs that he was being paid for.

There was an incident that took place in our kitchen years after the major renovations were completed. My sisters were making a chocolate cake when I was in high school. Pat had recently painted the kitchen a different color. One of my sisters was making the frosting and the other sister hit her arm. With that bump, chocolate frosting was splattered on the freshly painted white ceiling. I came home from being out with friends and out of the blue, the old man smashed me into a wall. I asked him what his problem was and he pointed to his precious ceiling. I saw the chocolate on the ceiling and asked what that had to do with me.

He said, "Your sisters said that you did that." I replied that "I wasn't even home so they were lying."

At that point, he could have considered the validity of my response but he was never too bright. He said "two against one so where should I punch you?" Then he started hitting me.

I raised a fist to defend myself and he said that he would love it if I hit back. I lowered my fist and went to my room when he was finished with my punishment.

That night, Pat started painting the entire kitchen ceiling. I happened to walk past him when he was in the laundry room and he gave me such a dirty look. I said to him, "You can give me all the dirty looks that you want, I didn't do anything. Ask your daughters what really happened and don't give me that lame excuse *two against one.*"

He had no response and there was no reason to pursue anything further since someone had already paid the price. The fact that this man didn't just paint over the small affected area boggles my mind. Instead, he painted the entire ceiling and wasted hours on this needless task. This story illustrates my point and shows what a perfectionist he was.

My kids have used crayons on our walls and actually put a hole in the ceiling in my current home. Did I hit anyone to mete out justice? No, instead I repaired the affected area. It took minutes to paint over something or to patch a wall. I moved on and enjoyed my kids. I am not good at giving out dirty looks anyway and I am not about to start now. My attitude is that a house is four walls and a home is what we make of it. In addition, everything is repairable or replaceable and there aren't any problems that we can't fix. These stories show the difference between me and my old man and the difference is quite stark. My wife sometimes wonders if I was adopted because I am very different from the rest of my family members. In addition, I am the antithesis of my old man.

The Control Factor

Bullies are scary. They rule with intimidation and fear. I have known many bullies in my lifetime. One trait that they all exhibit is the need to be controlling. They need to control every situation and it frustrates them when they lose control. In many situations, the bully is intelligent enough to manipulate others to maintain control. Some bullies are good enough actors that they are able to fool people into not seeing the truth about who they really are.

Pat was very controlling when I was growing up. He still is but the frustrating thing for him is that his control is dwindling as time goes on. His immediate family does not bother with him and that is by his own hand. Of course, he cannot admit this, and he uses the *Book of Excuses* to deflect the truth. Pat should have been a politician because he is such a good actor and is willing to lie. Pat is very believable and as such, he can manipulate the people around him. My mother, sisters, and I were unfortunate enough that he had a tight grip on all of us. When the time was right, we took off. That allowed us to finally remove the restraints that he had placed on all of us. It was quite liberating when we tasted freedom for the first time. We were then able to live our lives as the people who we really were, as opposed to who Pat allowed us to be.

Nothing screams control like the white glove test. My sisters and I were in elementary school at the time. This one winter Saturday comes to mind as we had just finished eating breakfast. Pat walked into the dining room and ran his fingers over the top of the door jamb in this room. He said "Marie, what is this?" My mother walked into the dining room and saw dust on his finger. He grabbed her by her hair and shoved his finger into her face. He then screamed "I want this entire house spotless by the time I get home. Get the kids to help you and I will check everything later."

We all looked at each other and then grabbed the vacuum and other cleaning products. We started dusting and cleaning because we knew that Pat would start hitting all of us if we did not comply with his demands. We spent our entire weekend cleaning a home that was already clean.

It was about this same period of time when Pat tried to teach me a lesson about leaving drops of urine on the toilet bowl rim. I was sound asleep when Pat came barging into my room. It was about 11:00 at night and he was getting ready to go to bed. He must have lifted the toilet seat and noticed drops of urine on the rim of the toilet bowl. That infuriated him, so he woke me up and grabbed me by one of my ears. He dragged me down the hall and into the bathroom as he yelled at me. He made me use toilet paper to wipe it up and he yelled when I took too much toilet paper. He told me that I needed to use two squares to clean the rim.

Stories like this stay with me to this day. I think about them and shake my head in disbelief. I would never even think about scolding my son for doing the same thing. When Diane and I used to visit Pat in his home years later, I would exact my revenge. I would purposely leave urine all over the toilet bowl rim whenever I used his bathrooms. In addition, I would lick my fingers and leave wet fingerprints all over his mirrors and expensive dining room armoire glass. Pat was always such a perfectionist, that this would definitely drive him nuts. He would clean the glass and mirrors and then I would do it again the next time. Diane would just laugh about it. Once Diane understood why I left fingerprints on his glass and mirrors, she became my co-conspirator. She would distract Pat and Joanne and this would allow me to walk throughout his house and leave my fingerprints everywhere.

By writing this book, I am putting the world on notice that I took my beatings and I survived. I am not justifying Pat's actions in any way. I dusted myself off and went on with my life. I made something of myself and didn't allow this prior treatment to hinder my life in any way. I did learn from Pat's abuse. I realized that I could not be the kind of man that Pat was. I could not be the kind of husband that Pat was. I certainly could not be the same type of father that Pat was. Pat influenced my life, but not in a positive way and not in the way that he intended. No one understands the trauma that our family was forced to endure. We can only explain it and even then people will not truly understand what we went through. No one can comprehend how Pat broke each one of us down, piece by piece. It was emotional, mental, and physical torture. I wouldn't wish this type of treatment on anyone. Whether intentional or not, it happened. Despite all of this, we plowed through. I, for one, never had any suicidal thoughts. I saw the light at the end of the tunnel and couldn't wait for the day when I could bust out and never look back.

My sisters and I were in the same type of situation. We were born into a household totally controlled by Pat. We did not know any better and didn't have a clue about how other people lived. I always assumed that other kids my age were being beaten by their fathers also. I assumed that other kids were being told how dumb that they were. I assumed that my friends were made to feel bad about themselves just like I was. Once I got a little older, these assumptions that I had made were proven to be wrong.

Every new day brought the possibilities of bullying in a variety of forms. The physical abuse was bad enough, as the bumps and bruises eventually healed. The mental abuse caused irreparable damage and stays with us forever. Do I get angry about the shit that we were compelled to endure? Yes, but taking it out on my loved ones serves no purpose at all. In addition, it is wrong. The ramifications of Pat's actions live with him today. He is lonely and bitter and can only blame himself. The sad truth is that he doesn't blame himself, but rather blames everyone else.

As a youngster, I began to wonder why God placed me in a home controlled by a bully that I trusted. Was this God's way of playing a cruel joke on me? Did I do something terrible and this was my punishment? A father is supposed to look out for his kids and protect them. Pat was not that kind of man. Pat only looked out for Pat. I never had privacy growing up. If I was home and not doing anything productive, Pat would find something for me to do.

All of the work that he forced me to do was useful for him and his agenda. When the garage door needed to be painted, Pat decided that his slave would strip off the old paint and then repaint it. He showed me how to use a gigantic acetylene torch that a twelve-year old boy should not be using. This was a dangerous tool and I could have blown myself up and taken the garage with me also. He would have been really upset with me if that had happened because he kept his motorcycle in that garage.

One hot summer day, I was using the torch and I noticed bees going into a hole in the garage. These bees were big and they formed a nest by drilling a hole in the wood. I was bored so I decided to see what would happen if I torched their nest. I applied the heat to the opening of the nest and they started to come after me. I was a madman as I defended myself with the torch. These bees couldn't fly without wings and the torch burned their wings off. Soon I had a collection of bees on the floor. I roasted them on the concrete. Then one bee attacked me and I dropped the torch as I ran away. The problem was that the torch almost blew up the tank and this could have been a real disaster. The lesson here is that children should not be left with dangerous equipment or tools because the results could be disastrous.

My mother, sisters, and I were just like those bees. We were as helpless as those wingless bees. Once we grew wings, we flew away. Pat never knew about my recklessness with the torch. I cleaned up all of the evidence as I didn't need another beating from Pat the bully. When Pat did come home into an empty house after we had all left, it must have felt like a really bad bee sting. As awful as that sounds, we needed to break away and live life the way it was supposed to be lived. We did just that and he eventually moved on as well.

Mean, Mean, Man

From the moment that each of my children were born, I fell in love with them. I was by my wife's side for each of their births. Diane was always very feminine and I always loved that about her. She always had her makeup, hair, and nails done perfectly. She was always dressed like a lady. In addition, she always carried herself very gracefully. In the past, I had been out with some women who looked like they just rolled out of bed. Others had mouths like truck drivers and at times they were very embarrassing. My wife is very refined and when she and I met, I knew that we were a perfect match and my days of being single were numbered. When she cooked for me, I knew that this girl was for me and that sealed the deal. In addition, her meatballs were better than I have ever tasted and I should know since I grew up in an Italian family. My philandering ways came to an end as soon as I met Diane.

Soon after Diane and I met, she wanted to stop by my office so that we could do the lunch thing. When she arrived, I introduced her to my co-workers. One of the women in the office must have noticed something because I overheard Jeannie say "Oh yeah, he's hooked." She was able to read the tea leaves from a female perspective and she nailed it with that comment. I didn't think much of that comment at the time, but in hindsight, I realize that Jeannie saw something that day and her female intuition told a tale. Diane and I then went to lunch.

When Marisa was born years later, my wife couldn't wait to dress this cupid doll up in feminine dresses and other outfits. Marisa looked adorable in those outfits and certainly played the part. We have photos of her pushing a baby carriage with our West Highland Terrier in the carriage. That day, Marisa actually dressed Cookie in a baby outfit and wheeled the carriage around the first floor of our home. Cookie was great with our kids and didn't have a bad bone in her body. When Joseph was about two years old, he stuck his finger up Cookie's butt and the dog just ran as fast and as far as she could. I guess that my son was curious about what that thing under her tail was so he touched it. My wife saw the whole thing and screamed. I came running because I thought that someone got hurt. Diane said to me "Oh my God. Joseph just stuck his finger up Cookie's butt." I lifted him over the sink and Diane proceeded to wash Joseph's hands until they were ready to fall off. He cried because she cleaned them so good. Thank God that he never did that again. That incident was traumatic for the entire family!

Both of my kids enjoyed playing with me when they were young. We used to play "*Socks*" in my bedroom. All of the socks in my underwear drawer were dumped on the floor and the two kids would team up against me. I would hide on one side of my bed and they would be on the other side. I would throw the rolled-up socks at them and the socks would bounce off their heads. The kids would team up against me and return fire. Sometimes the socks would hit someone in the eye, but that was rare. It never deterred either child from wanting to play. Some of the religious statutes in our bedroom bear scars from those days. To this day, St. Joseph is missing a piece of his head. We knocked over many things during those intense battles and the only one to complain was Diane.

Another game that we played was "*The BBQ.*" The kids didn't run away from me when it was their turn to be put on the *BBQ.* This game also took place in my bedroom. I would pick up each child by grabbing both hands with my left hand and both legs with my right hand. I would drop my child on the bed and make believe that I was slathering BBQ sauce on them. They would giggle and really enjoy themselves. I remember Joseph saying to me, "Daddy, it's my turn. Put me onto *the BBQ.*" They both were so cute when we played those games. My father was so stern that he never bothered to play anything with me. I decided a long time ago that I was not going to be that kind of father.

One night, Marisa wanted to be put on *the BBQ* and I told her no. I very rarely told my children no but I just couldn't do it this one particular time. She was mad at me and told me that I was a "mean, mean, man." Marisa stills calls me a mean, mean, man because she knows that it is not true. She also likes to bust my chops. Other times, she calls me *Pat* just to get a rise out of me. She knows that I am nothing like Pat but she says it anyway. We all get a good chuckle out of these little jabs that we throw around.

When I was a youngster, Pat would take us to Jones Beach in the summertime. We would go into the ocean but since he wouldn't allow us to bring sand into his car, we would then go into the big public swimming pool afterwards. He would make my sisters and I dive off the high diving board. Donna and I loved it and had no problem diving off that board repeatedly. My sister Sally was really scared to jump. On this beautiful hot summer day, all of the people at the pool witnessed a spectacle. Pat made Sally climb up the ladder to the diving board. Pat stood down below shouting at her to jump. She wouldn't jump and he yelled at her louder and more intensely. She was scared to jump, but she was petrified of her father. This went on for about ten minutes as he yelled at this eight-year old girl. She kept crying out, "No Daddy, I'm scared." It didn't help that there were hundreds of witnesses to this spectacle. The people at this pool saw what an asshole that this man truly was. I felt so sorry for my sister but we all knew what Pat was and we hated him for it. Sally eventually went down the ladder and did not jump into the pool. My mother tried to comfort her but my father made fun of her for the entire trip home to Queens.

I was always scared of heights and the old man knew this. His solution was to make me overcome my fears by putting me on ladders and roofs. We had an old garage on our property. It was not attached to the house. When it needed a new roof, Pat had me up on the roof with him. When I refused to climb up the ladder, he told me, "Get your ass up there now." I had no choice but to follow his orders or else he would have beat me until I complied with his wishes. I finally got onto the roof. We worked in the hot sun for hours and did the entire job in one day. At one point, my fear of heights took over when I was on the roof. I lost my balance and slid off the roof into our neighbor's yard. I fell into some bushes which helped to break my fall. Pat called me stupid and made me climb right back up onto the roof. Falling off a roof does not help you to overcome your fear of heights. I have fallen off roofs three times in my lifetime. Thankfully, those falls were only about ten to twelve feet and I survived each one of them.

When I was about twelve years old, Pat came up with a new ridiculous job to keep his slave laborer busy and out of trouble. It is called *"clean the gutters and while you are up there, wax the gutters because they are dirty."* These gutters were about thirty feet off the ground. I had to learn how to use an extension ladder and move it. I had to stick my hands into the gutters on both sides of the house. After I cleaned the inside of the gutters, I had to wax the outside of the gutters. Pat believed that white gutters should not have dirt and grime on them. Then I had to use a rag to wipe off the wax and make them look shiny and spiffy. He also made me wax the two air conditioners that we owned. Every summer, I was up on the ladder cleaning and waxing the gutters. I wound up doing this job about five years in a row. Had I fallen, I might not have survived the fall or I could have ended up in a wheelchair. Pat didn't care and was not concerned if my life was cut short or ruined. As long as his white gutters looked clean, he was happy. He was probably afraid that the *gutter police* might not like dirt on the gutters.

The home that I live in currently has beige vinyl siding with white trim and white gutters. Sometimes, I tease my son that he should go and wax my gutters. We laugh and he says, "like that would ever happen." AAG is a company that I use to clean my gutters. Whenever they get clogged, these guys come over. They assume the risk that I won't take and they are professionals. I wouldn't put my son's life in jeopardy now or ever. For the fifty bucks that it costs, it is worth every penny. We recently had a leaky gutter and this company replaced all of the gutters in the front. They put shiny new white gutters in place last year and now they have black streaks on them. I surely hope that the *gutter police* don't knock on my door!

I was eight or nine years old when Pat gave me the chore of cutting the lawn. I was kind of young to be doing such a dangerous job. When he provided a gas mower, I nearly cut my foot off. Thankfully, I only lost a sneaker. The shoe lace got wrapped in the lawn mower blade and nearly pulled my foot into the underside of the mower. Years later, he replaced the gas mower with an electric mower. One day, I ran over the electric cord and got a shock. I told him about it and he yelled at me and put black electric tape over the gash in the cord and made me finish the job.

Growing up in Whitestone, we had a dog who was very aggressive and crazy. Her name was Lady and she was kind of a bitch. She bit Donna in the face. Lady lived about fifteen years and died in our kitchen when we were eating dinner. Our home was robbed weeks earlier and the thieves must have given her a heart attack or beat her. She was never the same after that break in. Of course, the thieves were never caught. We buried her in our backyard under the spot that she would take daily naps. The spot that she was laid to rest was very picturesque as it was under this gigantic oak tree that has since been taken down. Lady loved my father, just like we all did. She also feared him and when she did something wrong, he beat the crap out of her. He would walk her late at night but he wouldn't use a leash. He thought that he had a magical spell over her and she would always listen to him. In the past, she had jumped out of the car window to attack other dogs. She also didn't listen to him during those nightly walks. One night, Lady attacked another dog as he walked her. Pat had to pull our thirty-pound dog off of the other dog, apologize, and drag Lady home. As soon as he got in the doorway, he threw her down the flight of stairs into the basement. She fell at least ten feet and survived the fall. I would be lying if I said that this only happened one time, it didn't. It kept happening over and over and each time he threw her down the stairs for not listening to him. One night, I said to him, "Why don't you use the leash?" He was so enraged that I challenged him that he hit me. Then I went downstairs to check on our dog who was shaking in fear. I am surprised that she never broke any bones during those falls. Perhaps if she was the perfect dog she would have had a better quality of life. All of us felt Pat's wrath, including a dog whose mental capacity was not as comprehensive as a human's. The stark reality was that you couldn't reason with this dog to prevent additional episodes from occurring. Nevertheless, she was a living, breathing creature of God who did not deserve the beatings that she endured.

We didn't deserve the beatings that we endured either. Donna rarely got beatings from my father, but he did hit her. She was his little princess as she was the youngest of his three children. The one time that I saw him hit her, she packed her bags and left the house. She was about seven years old and walking around the neighborhood with a suitcase. Eventually, she came home after several hours.

My sister Sally was another story. She did receive several beatings from Pat. They weren't as violent as my beatings, but he didn't seem to like her either. She and I had similar issues since we were both in his crosshairs at all times. I remember one beating that she took. It was a Friday night and we were having oatmeal for dinner. Like I said earlier, we were living in a neighborhood that was above my parent's means. Sally always had a big mouth and I often referred to her as the "town crier." She tasted the oatmeal and threw her spoon into the dish. Oatmeal spilled onto the table as she said, "I'm not eating this shit." Pat rose from his seat and kicked and punched her from the kitchen into the dining room. Then he continued pounding her until she was able to get away from him and escape to her bedroom which was upstairs. I had gotten up to try to help her but my mother grabbed me and told me to let her be. My mother knew that I would also be getting a beating from Pat if I intervened. To this day, Sally refers to Pat as "that guy." She could also call him a mean, mean, man.

Busting Out

I was such a geek when I attended elementary school and junior high school. I was always very compliant and had the necessary filters to keep my mouth shut most of the time. I felt that a change was needed once I graduated from these schools. I needed to re-invent myself and change my ways.

When I first arrived at the Bronx High School of Science, I wanted to be the cool kid from Queens. I gravitated towards a lot of the older kids and I would hang out with them before, during, and after school. My uniform was the same each day. It consisted of jeans, sneakers, and a tee shirt. It didn't matter if it was ninety degrees or ten degrees out. In the winter, I wore my leather bomber jacket and it lasted me for the four years that I attended this school. We would smoke pot and drink all sorts of alcohol. We would cut full days of school or just skip a class here or there. I had a blast in high school and I hung out with many of the girls that attended this school. Part of my persona was that I was a jock and I reaped many benefits because of this. I joined the swim team in my sophomore year. I swam for the St. Luke's swim team for all the years that I attended my two previous schools. I also swam for the Flushing Flyers swim team for many years. I did very well in all of the competitions and I took it to another level during my high school years. In my senior year, I was one of the co-captains of the Bronx Science swim team.

I appeared to be a very confident young man who attended one of the best schools in the country. I did all of my work and very rarely studied for tests. Despite all of the fun that I had, my grades were pretty good. Many of my teachers knew me well and liked me. Mr. English was my favorite teacher. He was also my guidance counselor. He taught several science classes that were my favorite classes. I was friendly with his son Donald. Mr. English started a program which was dedicated to the survivors of the Holocaust. Donald and I would run errands and help to get the Holocaust Center together. When we graduated, the Holocaust Center was located in part of the library and it was a success.

One day during Mr. English's class, I asked to be excused. I went to the cafeteria to get a drink and then went outside to talk to some of my friends. When I returned to class with a drink in hand, the entire class was laughing. Apparently, Mr. English had the entire class looking out of the window to see how long it would take me to appear in the school yard. Right on cue, I appeared and was hanging out and talking to many of my female friends. Sometimes, I would cut classes and get in a bind and Mr. English would provide guidance counselor passes to bail me out.

Mr. Henry was an English literature teacher who never liked me. He was nice enough to state that, "you will never make anything of yourself." He was an arrogant asshole who I didn't like very much. I used to drive him crazy when I brought bottle rockets to school. Mr. Henry's classroom was at the end of the hallway. I would go to the opposite end of the building, right near the staircase. I would light the bottle rockets on the floor and they would travel to the outside of Mr. Henry's classroom and explode. He would come out of the room to investigate and I would be long gone, having used the stairway to escape. Other times, I would light napkins filled with Sulphur powder outside of his classroom. These napkin packets would smell like the worst fart ever and the hallway would really smell badly. I would always time this prank with the ringing of the bell so that the kids in the school would have to change classes when the smell was very pungent. As smart as Mr. Henry thought that he was, he never even had a clue that I was the culprit.

Despite the confident façade that I presented, I was a totally different person when I was home. My sisters and I were good kids who were relaxed and living our lives when Pat was not home. Once he came home from work, our collective demeanors changed totally. None of us knew who he would attack mentally or physically because he was in a bad mood.

During the swim season, I was out of the house for about ten to twelve hours per day. Sometimes, I would rest in my bed when I got home because I was tired. If Pat caught me resting, he would find some bullshit job for me to do. The same logic was applied to my sisters and my mother. He believed that he would keep us busy and then we would stay out of trouble. The best thing for us to do was to not be home whenever he was home. I was constantly running away from my home so that I avoided him. He thought that I was working my lawn business or collecting lawn proceeds but a lot of times, I was just avoiding him.

I was fifteen years old when I began my sophomore year of high school. I would go to swim practice at DeWitt Clinton high school which was on the same gigantic block as our school. It is ironic that one of the worst schools in the city and one of the best schools in the city were both located on the same block. Both schools had a swim team and we shared their pool every morning.

One morning, I arrived for our 6:30 AM practice and none of my teammates were in the water. They were staring at a very large rat that was dead at the bottom of the pool. One of the kids on the Clinton team jumped into the pool and retrieved the carcass and dropped it in the garbage pail. Then we all went in the pool and began our practice. After practice, I was standing in front of Bronx Science talking with friends. The teacher who taught my second period mechanical drawing class saw me outside and when I didn't show up for his class, he knew that I cut his class. I don't remember his name, but he caught me in the hallway later that day. He questioned me as to why I missed his class. I replied that, "my father dropped me off at the bus stop late and I missed the bus." He knew that I was lying, but he let me go and I totally forgot about our conversation.

Later that evening, this teacher called my father to complain that I cut his class and then lied to his face. Pat got off the phone and was determined to rectify the situation. I was working on a term paper and sitting at my desk in my bedroom. Pat entered my room with a desk drawer in his hands that he had been fixing in his workshop. Pat slammed the desk drawer over my head with all of his might. The drawer shattered into pieces when it slammed into my skull. My desk was facing the window that overlooked our pool so I never even saw him coming. Pat was screaming and cursing at me about the fact that I cut class as he pulled me up off the floor. He punched and kicked me as he kept pounding on my head and body. This beating went on for at least five minutes and was the most brutal beating that I was ever subjected to. Then Pat threw me down two flights of stairs and into the basement. When he was finished beating me to a bloody pulp, Pat told me that I was to sleep on the cold and damp floor until further notice. I was also warned not to sleep on the old chair that our dog slept on. During the night, Pat would check on me to make sure that I was following his orders.

My sister Donna witnessed this brutal beating. Then she ran back into her room to avoid this animal as he completed his mission of teaching me a lesson. She saw me flying down the first flight of stairs and Pat didn't care if he broke my neck or some other bones. He continued beating me and then kicked me down the second flight of stairs until I ended up on the basement floor.

The next day, I woke up bruised and battered and he forced me to go to school. It didn't matter that I was sore and had trouble moving. He needed me to go to school so that I could apologize to the teacher who started it all. I wonder if this teacher felt badly when he found out that Pat beat the shit out of me because of his phone call. I only mentioned it to him and the dean when this teacher caught me later in the semester cutting his class again.

I survived the worst beating of my life. It was dished out by Pat the bully who exacted his pound of flesh for the minor offense of cutting a class. My kids have cut classes and Diane and I laughed about it afterwards. If Pat thought that he was teaching me a lesson, he was dead wrong. He just made me hate him more and I was determined to not get caught next time. Instead of cutting individual classes, I just cut the entire day. I made sure not to show my face in the front of the building before school. Then I would produce an absence note that I fraudulently signed on behalf of my parents. The report cards were given to us twice a year and they indicated how many school days that I missed each semester. I would change the amount of days absent, using an eraser, and then spill hot chocolate on it so it was not legible. Pat would ask me about the smudges and buy my bullshit answer hook, line, and sinker. As a teenager, I was able to run circles around this man and he never even had a clue.

I confronted Pat about the beatings that I endured, years later. He claimed that he only hit me twice and I deserved it both times. When I asked him why he hit me, he responded that, "you cut school." I then asked "what was the other time?" and he couldn't answer the question. I understand that those "two times" took place decades earlier but he couldn't remember the specifics. My response was simply that, "I can remember getting beaten two times in one day."

The truth about Pat was that he always had a chip on his shoulder about me. He always targeted me, which is a common thing that bullies do. He was relentless and never really eased up on me. Living under his roof was depressing and uncomfortable. All of us felt his wrath. We suffered in silence and the damage that he did to all of us still exists to this day. It truly was an atmosphere that caused damage to us internally. Pat wanted people to think that he was the best husband and father and that he had the perfect family. We were always on our best behavior and if we weren't, we would be on the receiving end of a beating. This was designed to intimidate and warn us that more pain could be inflicted if we did not conform to his wishes. He ruled with an iron fist, just like his old man did. The façade that he presented was so convincing that everyone was fooled. **It was so good that even he was fooled!**

I always said that Pat was "an appearance person." I have known many people who can be characterized this way but the truth is that they are phonies. Pat's "alternate reality" really slapped him in the face when he came home from work one day and his family and our belongings were gone. He was such a miserable prick that we had to make the moving arrangements quietly because he would have interfered with our attempts to move out.

The title of this chapter is "busting out." I was referring to me growing up and becoming the person that I am today. I had lived my first eighteen years in this household under Pat's thumb. We had our arguments and we did not see eye to eye on many issues. I was becoming more vocal and less cooperative with him as I got older. My independence was making me more of a man and once I completed high school, Pat's thumbprint was quickly fading. In addition, I towered over him and he knew that if he raised a fist to hit me, I would not capitulate. The last time that he ever hit me was when I turned eighteen. I drove him to Brooklyn and nearly rear-ended the car in front of my car. I hope he enjoyed punching me in the face that day because that was the last time that he ever touched me in anger.

Everything was coming to a head in the summer of 1980. There was a light at the end of our tunnel. We were moving out of this house and away from the bully who had victimized each and every one of us for what seemed like an eternity. Some of us were targeted more than others and that is not meant to minimize anyone's suffering. It was at this time that I moved out of the house. I was not willing to put up with this arrogant asshole's bullshit any longer. One day, Pat and I argued about his ridiculous and arbitrary five-day lawn schedule and I drove away. I didn't speak to Pat for more than one year.

It was probably at that time when he realized that his targets were planning their exit strategy. This bully was losing his grip on all of us. We were all busting out and it was just a matter of time before it happened. What good is a bully if he has no victims?

A Victim of his own Quirkiness

I always said to my wife that "my father is a lonely, bitter old man, and he always will be." He is a victim of his own quirkiness. I spent eighteen years of my life living under Pat's roof and it was not always pleasant. Most of my good memories took place when Pat was not home. My sisters can attest to this fact because they felt the same way.

Pat does not know how to interact with people on a personal level. Whenever he went to a social function, he needed to reach for the booze in order to loosen up. The last time that I sat with him at a bar, he seemed very comfortable there. He always bragged that whenever he and his wife went to Caribbean resorts, he always paid for top shelf liquor. If someone needs liquor to be human and to be able to interact with people, this can be a real problem. When I was growing up, Pat only drank with his dinner. He would have one or two beers or glasses of wine. Now, he begins his drinking at lunchtime. When Pat was working, he would come home with one gallon jugs of red wine that were made by some of the Italian construction workers. This wine was very potent as the Perulo boys and I would find out.

When we were bored and no one was home at my house, I would go into the closet by the front door and grab one of those bottles. The three of us would chug the wine and not leave any evidence of our crimes. We would be very happy every time Pat got a new bottle of the "good stuff." I got in trouble for a lot of shit in my day, but Pat never caught me with that one.

Teddy, Henry, and I would go to this one grocery store that never checked our identifications. We would buy cheap cans of beer from this local store. We started this when we became teenagers. I remember those days as if it was yesterday. The three of us also raided their father's liquor cabinet. We tried everything that Steve Perulo had stashed in his house. Then Henry would fill the bottles with water to make up for what we drank. We never got caught although my father complained that Steve would water down his liquor! The one time that I saw my old man get sick was in Steve's driveway. He puked all over the gravel and I laughed. To this day, Pat claims that he never got drunk. I reminded him of that party and the deposit that he left in Steve's driveway.

When the three of us were on summer break, we always took a bus to Jones Beach in Long Island. In preparation for this beach day, Henry and I went to the local supermarket. We paid a guy to buy a case of beer for us because we were too young to purchase alcohol. We brought it to Henry's house and to our surprise, Steve was home. We threw the case of beer in the bushes and went into the house. Steve demanded that we give him the beer. Apparently, he saw our transaction outside of the supermarket and was going to teach us a lesson. Henry gave the case of beer to his father and he sat there and drank it all in front of us. The next day, we got on the bus with a couple of sodas and my boom box.

Pat always had the view that it was his way or the highway. This stubbornness has had a definite impact on his life. I believe that in life, you must not rely on Plan A only. I have always been willing to adapt Plan A or even shift gears and try Plan B or Plan C. Perhaps, Pat's way of doing things worked for him in the 1950s and the 1960s, but it certainly does not fly in this day and age.

I understand that Pat is the captain of his own ship. I don't have a problem with that kind of thinking. If you are living your life a certain way and it is not working out for you, then maybe you should consider an alternative. We had a family unit that consisted of five people. One by one, Pat pushed everyone away. Now he has no one. He can pull out any excuse that he wants to use, but the truth is that he has no one to blame but himself. The problem is that he is too arrogant to admit that he was wrong and by not admitting fault, he is not willing to fix the problem. As a result, he will always be alone.

The end result is what counts. I always tell my wife that to get from Point A to Point B is not always a straight line. My wife and I have had struggles with both of our kids when they were teenagers.

Marisa's story exemplifies my point perfectly. Marisa was always a great kid, until she turned thirteen. We never had a problem with her and then Grandpa Sam died at the age of seventy-one. We all loved Diane's father and enjoyed his company. Sam was a successful businessman and he loved his family more than anything. Marisa was his first grandchild and he was so excited when she was born. He and I looked at Marisa in amazement when she was getting cleaned up after coming into this world. At that point, she was less than an hour old and we watched the nurses bathe her and put her hospital infant outfit on. Sam was the patriarch of the family and was not shy about giving his opinion to anyone and everyone. We all respected him and he and I worked in insurance. He and I had that in common, among other things. I can remember Marisa sitting on the kitchen table as a two-year old with Sam holding her upright. She was putting clips in his hair and he was enjoying every minute of it. The photos that we have tell a story and it is a really special one. For the first thirteen years of Marisa's life, she had Grandpa Sam living in the same neighborhood and he passed by every day to get a glimpse of his grandkids and say hello. Then Sam died suddenly. We rushed him to the hospital one night and he was gone by morning. We were all devastated but Marisa took it especially hard. This is when our troubles with our daughter began.

One year after losing her grandfather, Marisa was struck by a Chevy Blazer. She was crossing a street right near our home with several local kids. A man was driving his truck and hit her as a pedestrian. She crossed the street mid-block and this man was driving too fast through a school zone. She was transported to a trauma hospital and one week later was on the operating table. She had a left ankle fracture which needed plates and screws. She also needed plates and screws in her face and head due to multiple facial and skull fractures. She received great medical treatment and her recovery was tough but she pulled through just like a trooper. She is very lucky that Diane cared for her open wounds and prevented any infections.

We had our difficulties with this teenager who was very sassy and was not shy in blasting all of us for nonsense. Marisa was very disrespectful to my wife and I but we all hung in there for many years. Then all of this shit just disappeared once she went to college and grew up. We dealt with her the best way that we could. Today, Marisa is a beautiful young woman who works for an insurance brokerage and is doing well. She has her four-year old Pit Bull and a boyfriend and I will be very sad when she moves out to start her new life.

One Sunday when Marisa was about sixteen years old, Pat and Joanne came over for dinner. Marisa was giving me a hard time about something and was very disrespectful. I talked to my daughter very calmly and eventually told her to go upstairs. My father sat across from me in our dining room. In the middle of Marisa's bullshit, he chimed in and said, "you should rap her in the mouth." I responded by stating, "mind your own fucking business." I embarrassed my old man in front of my in-laws, but I put him in his place.

This little episode between me and my father reminded me of the beating that my sister Sally received when we were kids. Pat's way of dealing with such issues involved violence but I didn't want to be that kind of father. Like I said earlier, my wife and I dealt with our kids in our own fashion and it worked for us. Both of our kids do not fear us. Instead they love and respect their parents and they recognize what good parents we are and always were. It also helps that they see how other people live and treat their children.

Pat was always very stern. He was never fun to be around and the fact that he didn't have much of a personality didn't help the situation. When I had to work with him, I was very uncomfortable being around him. The silence was deafening. If he wanted to be funny, it was always at someone else's expense.

Pat installed a pool in our backyard when we were in elementary school. It was an above ground pool and it was sixteen feet wide and thirty-two feet long. We then built a deck with a nice bench and the yard was beautifully landscaped around this pool. Like everything that involved Pat, he was fanatical about how everything looked. I bore the brunt of the maintenance for his dream yard. In addition to cutting the lawn, I was responsible for keeping the pool in tip top shape. Every year, I had to sand down the deck and then stain it.

Pat very rarely went in the pool. I remember being in the pool with my sisters one summer day and my father jumped in. He must have been pissed off at me for something. This was very common for him. He came over to me and pushed my head under the water and wouldn't let me come up for air. I was struggling to get free and actually started to swallow water. Then he let me go and I choked as I gasped for air once I was released from his grasp. He thought that the entire episode was funny. Whenever he did go in the pool, I stayed far away from him. His actions were so unnecessary and certainly uncalled for. He always wanted to make me fear him and when I was young, it worked very well.

Frances was our maternal grandmother. We called her Nanny and we all have fond memories of her. Her garden apartment was about a mile from our home in Whitestone. I would go to her home with my bicycle and lock it on the bicycle rack that was located by the front stairs. My mother and I would go to visit her on weekends when we needed to get away from Pat. Whenever Marie had a fight with her husband, she would get in her car and go to her mother's apartment to get away from him. She actually did this a lot. Pat knew this and then he would disconnect her car battery so that she couldn't run away from him. He was so vindictive, cunning, and calculating.

When I was seventeen, I used Nanny's car to learn how to drive. She owned a gold 1969 Mustang. This car was a two-door sedan that was small but it had an eight-cylinder engine. This little car had so much power and it was a great car. My sisters and I passed the New York State road tests by using this car. We all loved that Mustang. It wasn't really used much because Nanny worked in Manhattan and took buses and trains to go to and from work.

Uncle Anthony was Nanny's son. When he was in between girlfriends he would crash at Nanny's apartment and sleep on the couch. He got good use out of the Mustang until he totaled it getting off the Whitestone Bridge. Nanny then replaced the Mustang with an old lady vehicle and he totaled that car also. I didn't care because I never liked that replacement car. I was upset that the Mustang was gone. Uncle Anthony stayed with Nanny for less than a year and then found another girlfriend and moved back to the Bronx.

When I was turning eighteen, I needed a car to finish my last year of high school. Pat picked out a 1969 Dodge Dart. He took me to see the car and he checked out the car. He told me to "pay the man." I gave the seller eight one-hundred-dollar bills and we drove the car home. I thought that the car was ugly and didn't really want it but Pat made up his mind so I was stuck with it.

Pat needed some body work done on his motorcycle and, of course, he couldn't get it done at a local shop. He found someone in Brooklyn to do the work. He needed a ride to the shop when the repairs were done. I drove him to the shop in my Dodge Dart. I was always uncomfortable with this man and I would talk to him to kill the silence. On this one afternoon, I was very chatty. I took my eyes off the road for one second and when I looked up, the traffic was stopped. I slammed on the brakes and avoided hitting the car in front of us. Pat was so enraged that he punched me in my jaw as he sat in the passenger seat. He yelled at me and said, "you could have killed me."

When we arrived home several hours later, Pat took my keys away and told me that I was not "capable of being a safe driver and shouldn't be on the road." My crime here wasn't so egregious, but Pat was punishing me once again. The funny thing is that all new drivers need to learn from their mistakes. I paid for the car myself and I was paying the insurance so Pat had no right to take my car keys away. I was forced to take the bus to school for two weeks until my sentence was served.

Pat's actions (when I almost rear-ended the car in front of us) were really over the top. I have been in this situation with my children when I was teaching them to drive. There was never a reason to hit my kids or verbally abuse them. It was a learning process. Marisa bought her Honda when she turned seventeen; the driving rules in Long Island are different than in New York City. I told her, "you are going to get your bumps and bruises as a new driver." Diane and Marisa thought that my comments were unnecessary and insulting. I defended myself by saying that "all new drivers make mistakes and must learn from those mistakes."

As time went on, I was proven right. First Marisa backed into a fire hydrant and damaged her rear bumper. Marisa and her ditzy girlfriend thought that the incident was funny as they drove away. Then one night, Diane and I received a midnight phone call that someone ran a red light and knocked her front bumper off. At 1:00 AM that morning, I was at the scene talking to the police officer about the car that had hit her Honda and fled the scene. Then there was the time that she hit a car in a parking lot. I could go on and on about her comprehensive and collision losses. Each and every issue that she had was handled appropriately and I never needed to scold my daughter. She felt bad enough about all of these situations and I assured her that "cars are replaceable but people are not."

Pat's comments that I could have killed him really revealed what he thought about himself. There was never any doubt in my mind that he was always a selfish man and a narcissist. I was always treated like a second-class citizen but that comment is very telling. He should have said that, "you could have killed us." It also would have been better if he discussed my mistake with me instead of punching me in the face. That is how I would have handled that situation but I am not Pat. Then again, Pat was never a good communicator and never even tried to be. His inability to communicate with his family was one of the factors that cost him his family.

In reflecting back on my life at home with the old man, I realize that Pat has never sacrificed one thing for any of his family members. His selfishness was always there but we never saw it at the time. Pat had thousands of dollars stashed under the floorboards in our attic. My sisters found it one day and they would go into the attic and help themselves. They knew that if Pat found out that they were using his cash, my mother would find out and question where that money came from. Pat probably never knew that some of that money was missing because he never moved his hiding place.

I was talking with my wife recently and I told her that if she or my kids needed a kidney from me, I wouldn't even hesitate to have the surgery and provide it. I'm not a selfish person but my old man is. If he was on the Titanic when it was sinking, he would make sure that he got on a lifeboat. It wouldn't matter if he left his wife or kids on that sinking ship as long as he was rescued. Perhaps we can put that on his headstone when the end comes.

My son bought a car and I didn't tell him that bumps and bruises are part of life. He learned several months ago that you have to keep your eyes on the road and pay attention at all times. He recently hit a car in the rear and the three people in that car claim that they were injured and have filed lawsuits. Like I said earlier, all new drivers need to learn a lot of things and they will only get that experience as they put more miles under their belts. It should also be noted that I did not punish my son at all. He was without a car for one week while his Jeep was being repaired. If he needed to go somewhere, he used my car.

When Joseph was enrolled in the driver's education class, I had to attend a meeting at the high school with him. I attended the same meeting with my daughter years earlier. Joseph drove me to the meeting and we entered the building. I asked the security guard, "Is this where the strippers are?" The guard started laughing and so did I. I looked over at my son and he was mortified. He told me that he would never go anywhere with me ever again. I thought that my comment was really funny but it was wasted on a teenager with no sense of humor. Then I fell asleep during that boring meeting.

We are all different people. My father is about as funny as the telephone book. He has no personality and he can only loosen up after a couple of drinks. I always try to make people feel comfortable and I also try to be funny without making fun of anyone. I don't need alcohol to be at ease with people. I always try to use situations to teach my children. That car accident my son was involved in has left him with a lasting memory that he does not want to ever repeat. In addition, he wasted an entire day just trying to get his car home. It took three hours to get his Jeep off the parkway and then he needed another tow truck to get his car to a body shop in our neighborhood.

Pat always had a fear of being alone. He was married to his second wife for about thirty years. The exact situation that he feared has come to fruition as Joanne passed away before him. Now, Pat is all alone. When Joanne came into the family in the 1980s, Pat was determined to do things differently. He was not going to go down the same path that he did with his past family. He elevated his wife to God-like status, but it was obvious that things were going to be done her way. Pat was always a cold individual and he found someone just as cold as he was. Joanne had a plan and she began to implement it immediately. She was looking for the motherlode and Pat had money and assets, which she wanted.

Joanne started working on my sisters first. She would get Pat to buy her expensive jewelry and then she would flaunt it in my sisters' faces. Joanne would say, "look at the ring that your father bought for me." They would go home and tell my mother about the expensive jewelry that Joanne received. That would piss off my mother and both sisters because he never bought any jewelry for Marie. There is an old saying that "the first wife walks and the second one rides." Pat never bought my mother anything expensive and he never bought her a new car. He always purchased used cars that he fixed up and gave to Marie. This new wife needed expensive cars as well. Every couple of years, he bought her a new Lexus or Mercedes. Joanne seemed to be living "the life." Pat and Joanne lived in Middle Village, which is the neighborhood where Joanne lived before getting re-married. The house that they lived in was nice but not good enough for Joanne. Pat had no mortgage on that house and he owned it outright before he was married. Joanne convinced him that the house was too small and they needed to move to Whitestone. Like a little puppy, Pat did as Joanne wanted. One night she got drunk at a party and said to a family member, "I do everything for Pat and I mean everything." There is a song called "Gold Digger" and my kids used to play it whenever the subject of Joanne came up. We would all laugh as the song played. My kids certainly hit the nail on the head.

Everything was falling into place. Joanne effectively eliminated my sisters from the picture, was getting expensive pocketbooks, jewelry, and cars, and now she lived in an expensive neighborhood. Then they joined the Robinwood Association and rubbed elbows with the elite of Queens. They went to parties with successful professionals but the only problem was that as soon as Pat and Joanne opened their mouths, people knew their secret. These uneducated people could barely put a sentence together but they lived in the neighborhood and were living the life.

Not everything was perfect for Joanne. She was extremely jealous of my mother. It was as if she was competing with a ghost. Marie was always there in the background, although she was not in Joanne's face. My father always knew that his daughter, Donna, was beautiful and he had not seen her in years. Joanne was also jealous of Donna because if Pat did bump into her, he would never stop blabbing about her. Marisa was always respectful to Joanne and Pat idolized her as well. So now, there were three women who were on Joanne's forever shit list. Her jealousy just ran so deep.

Joanne spent years putting herself into a situation where she would inherit everything when Pat kicked the bucket. She was ten years younger than Pat and he had lung issues from working with asbestos. He collected a lot of money from the asbestosis that he contracted from his job. He was well compensated for his illness. Joanne was reaping the rewards of his settlements. Then the irony of life stepped in, Joanne died at the age of sixty-five.

My father always told me that "Joanne was a good girl." He said this because she went to church on Sundays. I once knew an attorney who went to church every Sunday and everyone thought that he was such a good Catholic. It turned out that he was having an affair with one of his employees for many years and he had many people fooled. Well, Joanne had my father fooled. He was never the sharpest tool in the shed, so she probably didn't have to work too hard at that part.

My wife and I felt badly that Joanne passed away at such a young age. I never thought of her as an upstanding citizen. She pushed away Pat's three kids and all the while, she told everyone that she kept trying to get Pat to reach out to his kids. My sisters and I saw through the façade. I believe that Pat is responsible for his fate because he allowed his second wife to destroy his family relationships, which were very tenuous anyway. Either he was that stupid or his quirkiness would not allow him to compromise and spend time with his kids and grandkids.

Years before Joanne passed away, my wife had a discussion with Pat. Diane explained that if Joanne couldn't come over to our house that he should come over during the week by himself. She also told Pat that Joanne was cold to our kids and they felt that. They were not Joanne's flesh and blood and that was very obvious. The solution was for him to come over during the week when Joanne was at work. Using this solution, he could spend time with his grandkids and Joanne would not be subjected to our dogs which she claimed were the reason for her allergy problems. Pat was obviously upset that my wife told the truth and was honest enough to suggest a viable solution. After Pat shared the conversation with his wife, there were now two people in Whitestone who were mad at us. This situation played perfectly into Joanne's hands. After she got rid of Pat's son, there was no one left to get in her way.

My conclusion is that Pat is a victim of his own quirkiness. He was also played very skillfully by his second wife who did an excellent job of eliminating all of the competition. My sisters just walked away quietly. I hung in there for many years because I wanted to be a good son. Perhaps, I was seeking my father's approval. Once in a while, he would throw out a little bone for me when he stated. "ya done good junior."

There is a saying that "people make plans and God laughs." Joanne spent years positioning herself to inherit all of Pat's assets and it was all for naught. Pat did his best to accumulate as much money as possible and it did not matter who was hurt during his quest for wealth. In the end, Joanne is six feet under and Pat is all alone. He has nobody. He has three nephews and their families, one cousin, and all the scotch that he can afford. I find this to be very sad for him but he is a very quirky guy. Not even the Pope would be able to convince Pat to change his ways.

Guilty - But with a Good Excuse

In the 1980s, there was a woman who cut off her husband's penis. Afterwards, she was arrested and went to trial for this terrible assault on her husband's manhood. It hurts me just thinking about it! This reminds me of a gag that we pulled when I was in school. When we had substitute teachers, they would pass around an attendance sheet and we would have to write down our names. Inevitably, someone in the class would then write their name as Dick Hertz. The teacher would read the list out loud and when she came to this name all hell would break loose. The teacher would say, "Whose Dick Hertz?" All of the boys would respond, "Mine does." These teachers never learned and fell for the same gag time and time again.

When that famous 1980s case went to trial, the defense was **Guilty - But with a Good Excuse.** The excuse in the instant case was that the victim would beat his wife and one day she went to bed with a knife and did the unthinkable. After this defense was used effectively, many people used the guilty with extenuating circumstances excuse. Of course, the situations were all different. This defense was meant to make the jury feel sorry for the accused and sometimes it worked. I can remember using this defense as a child and young adult, however I never killed or maimed anyone. My thinking was that I would try to explain myself whenever I was in trouble for something. I felt that it couldn't hurt to try.

The teacher who caught me cutting his class and called my father previously actually caught me a second time. He dragged me to the dean's office because he wanted justice. The dean informed me that he was going to call my father. My reply was, "if you do that, I will not be able to go home. The last time you called him, he beat me and threw me down two flights of stairs. I will not be able to go home if you make that call." Both men decided to let me slide for that minor cutting class offense. I guess that I shed a different light on my situation by stating the truth about my old man. In today's environment, teachers and schools cannot get away with letting information like this go unchallenged. The dean's response should have been to report this abuse to social services. At least, his conscious would have been clear had something happened after my revelation. The school's liability would have been minimized or perhaps even eliminated had they done the right thing at that time.

The social services scenario would have only made my situation worse since my father is a vindictive man. Some New York City employee with a clipboard would have shown up at our home. He or she would have evaluated the home environment and interviewed all of the people in our home. If we would have spoken the truth, perhaps the bureaucracy would have taken Pat's kids away from him. We probably would have lied to the investigator so that Pat's retribution was minimized. If Pat's secret had been exposed, he would have killed me. Since he was an appearance person, the embarrassment alone would have driven him to abuse me worse than ever. He is a good actor and he would have been able to deny any and all charges in a believable fashion.

Pat's brother was not so lucky. Uncle Phil had three boys. When his oldest son was in school, a teacher noticed bruises on his arm. The teacher asked Danny to remove his shirt and he did. This teacher saw many bruises on his back. She showed the principal and they promptly notified the authorities. The culprit was Aunt Lidia who hit her kids on a regular basis. The investigators kept tabs on my uncle and his home but the kids remained in the home. My cousin Danny never told me about this situation, but his wife was eager to explain the situation to my wife at a party several years ago. Danny and I then had a short discussion about the abuses that we endured over the years.

As an adult, I did confront Pat about some of his actions. His responses were very predictable. Deniability was always his first response and if he was not successful with that tact, he would use the **Guilty – But with a Good Ex-**

cuse Defense. This was his response when I confronted him about hitting my mother with a 2 x 4 over her head, neck, and back. He denied my allegation all together. When Marie's brother served Pat with the divorce paperwork in 1980, my Uncle Anthony asked him about the beatings that were referenced in the paperwork. Those allegations were listed under the "irreconcilable differences" section of the paperwork and my Uncle looked at that section first. Pat swore up and down that he never touched Marie or her kids. Years later, I told Pat that he stole my childhood because he wouldn't let me hang out with my friends on weekends. He always had work for me to do and that was frustrating for me. His reply was, "I needed your help and couldn't do it without you." There is that damn excuse again!

A perfect example of my childhood being stolen from me was when I was thirteen and my sisters were sent to sleep-away camp. One summer morning, he pulled me out of bed at 6:30 AM. He brought me into their bedroom. I remember his words to this day. He said, "rip this wall down and when I get home, it had better be all cleaned up. Use the bucket to dump all of the plaster by that tree out there. I don't want to see even one nail left." I knew to get the job done as he ordered or else there would have been hell to pay. The next day, I ripped down the next wall and then the next. Taking down the ceiling was the messiest job. At night, we loaded the debris into our car and went to the local supermarket and dumped all of the crap into their dumpsters.

When I confronted Pat about the beatings that I endured, he used the *Book of Excuses*. With a straight face, he stated, "I hit you twice and you deserved it both times." My response was, "Yeah, I can remember getting beaten twice in one day." I then asked him what I did to deserve such beatings and he couldn't adequately answer the question. I embarrassed him in front of my in-laws and he called his wife and informed her that they were leaving.

Pat would have preferred to deny that he ever hit me at all but he knew that I would never have let that slide. His next option was the one that he chose to use which was **Guilty - But with a Good Excuse**. This confrontation was probably the one that broke the camel's back. Our relationship really never recovered after that. We still got together but the strained atmosphere was certainly evident.

I remember helping Pat work in his house in Middle Village in the late 1980s. He had just finished painting the hallway on the main level. His new wife leaned an ironing board on the freshly painted wall. I didn't think that it was a big deal since the ironing board had rubber feet on it and they did not damage the wall at all. I saw him grab Joanne and twist her arm as he pushed her into the wall. I guess that his actions were justified since her crime was so egregious! Had I not been there, perhaps she would have ended up with more than just bruises on her arm. So much for the honeymoon phase of their marriage! I suspect that he bullied and abused Joanne just like he did to all of his family members. We always noticed bruises on her arms and once she wore dark sunglasses and refused to take them off in our house.

I can certainly use this guilty analogy to apply to my actions as well. As an adult, I laced into my father with the truth. I told him that he was a prick to me. I explained why he was a prick. As I look back, he may not have really accepted what I said. For many years after I spoke these words, he would ask me if I had anything to tell him. I knew that he wanted me to recant my prick statement. I would confidently reply that I had nothing to say. I would not be true to myself if I lied and told him what he wanted to hear. I was guilty of telling the truth to his face and he could never get over that fact. I guess that I was **Guilty - But with a Good Excuse.**

I Am Son of Prick

The dictionary describes a prick as an obnoxious individual who is worthy of contempt. It points out that a prick is usually a man. I called my father a prick to his face as we sat on a bench in the backyard of my first house. I did not consult the dictionary before I uttered those words because I knew what a prick was in practical terms. I also knew that Pat was the biggest prick that I had ever known in my entire life. Should I have called Pat a prick to his face? After all, he had just treated me to a very expensive steak dinner at a steakhouse in Great Neck. That statement exemplifies who I am as an individual. I have no qualms about speaking the truth and I never have. Our conversation lasted about two hours and I hit Pat with one truth bomb after another. I did not hold anything back. I had nothing to lose. I was giving Pat a chance to come back into our lives for the second time. I was under the impression that he wanted to be in our lives and that he would not waste this opportunity. As I later learned, I was wrong. He was Mr. Prick and he always will be.

Why was I in such a generous mood? It was because his mother had just died and I felt that this was something that she would have wanted. I loved Grandma Nancy and she was always very good to me. I wouldn't want to ever disappoint her. I also felt that I should be a good son. In addition, my wife and I had recently welcomed our second child into our family. Joseph was born about one year earlier and Pat had no idea that he was a grandfather for the fourth time in his life. I wanted to share my joy with a family member who I felt deserved another chance. If I were in Pat's shoes, I would have taken that gift and run with it. I am not Pat and he evidently did not accept this gift graciously. Like I said earlier, Pat was not the sharpest tool in the shed!

It is important to understand the context of my statement to the old man. He had just stated to me that he "could see the hatred" in my eyes when I looked at him. I felt the need to explain why I hated him.

I said to him, "I had hatred in my eyes because you were such a prick to me growing up. I was a good kid and never caused one ounce of trouble for you. I was compliant and did everything that you asked of me. What did I get for it? I was always the target of your rage. You beat the crap out of me constantly and I even got beatings for things that I didn't do. Nothing that I ever did was good enough for you. It was as if you hated me for the direction that your life took. In addition, you stole my childhood from me. I couldn't even hang out with my friends on the weekends because you always had work for me to do."

Pat's biggest problem with my response was with the prick reference. He said that "ninety-seven guys worked for me and no one ever called me a prick." I later debunked that answer because no one ever had the balls to call him a prick to his face. In addition, he did not have ninety-seven guys working for him. He was not a supervisor and not one person ever worked for him other than me.

Pat continued responding by stating that he needed my help to get things done in the house and on jobs that he picked up to make extra money. He was also nice enough to explain that he loved me and was so happy when I was born. He even bought cigars and handed them out at work. When my children were born, I didn't buy cigars so I guess that I didn't love my children! Thank God that I don't think the way that this man does. It has served me well to be my own thinker, even if my views are outside of the main stream.

In the end, results are very important. My father had three children and none of us felt any love from this cold man who called himself our father. That was something that was lacking in our lives and we carried that into adulthood. I was okay with growing up like this as it was all that I knew. My mother tried her best to make up for Pat's coldness. If it was not for her efforts to be affectionate with her kids, who knows how we would have ended up. I am not saying that we would be in jail or on death row, but you never know. Without Marie's love and support, we might have grown up really messed up.

I have known many women in my lifetime. Many of them had "daddy issues" and were looking for love in all the wrong places. Diane was not one of those women because her father was a stable parent and a good man. Parents are given a golden opportunity to raise their children and foster good relationships with their kids. Based on my experiences, many fathers don't use those opportunities to love their children the way that they need to be loved. As a result, many children grow up with mixed feelings and sometimes carry those issues for their entire lives. I don't know if my sisters had daddy issues or not. If they did, it was no fault of their own. I can't speak for my sisters, but Pat did not show any love to me when I was growing up. I couldn't ask him for advice because if I did he would attack me with it like he had done in the past. He provided zero guidance to me growing up, but I did just fine in life. I was able to do things on my own and get advice from people who I respected and felt comfortable speaking with. I was smart enough to go it alone and it worked for me. I was able to overcome his deficiencies as a parent and learn from my experiences. I feel that this made me a stronger individual.

My mother told me that Pat used to kiss me when I was very young. He used to hug me and enjoy his son. I saw photos when I was young and he looked like he was enjoying his growing family. Then, when I was about four years old, he stopped being affectionate with me. My mother questioned him about that and he really couldn't answer her question adequately. He turned into this cold, stern, and miserable individual. Could it have been that life was catching up with him? Was he not happy? Was he homophobic? The only way to get a decent answer would be if a forensic pathologist was to examine his brain!

The analogy that I can use to explain this oddity in relation to my life is as follows:

If a person has good vision and then loses that vision, they will know what they are missing. A person who is blind at birth, will not truly know what they are missing.

I was like the person who was born blind. Pat was cold to me from early on, so I did not yearn for his affection since I could not remember a time when he was a warm and loving person. Pat was not this great, loving parent who spent a lot of time with me and who changed suddenly. He was just some guy who lived with us and constantly broke my balls. I resented him for the better part of my first eighteen years. Once I moved out of his home, that resentment lessened over time. Now, it is a non-factor as I moved on with life and put Pat in my rear-view mirror. I very rarely give Pat much thought at all. He made his choices and must live with the consequences.

I was always the type of person who would learn from other people's mistakes. In fact, I think that it is one of my best qualities. My grandmothers would say "fool me once, shame on you. Fool me twice, shame on me." If I did not learn from Pat's foolish mistakes and I repeated his mistakes then I would deserve what was thrown at me. I didn't follow in his footsteps. I created my own and I am proud of my choices. I am affectionate with my kids and always was. We had a blast when the kids were young. I would play with my children and we would have lots of fun. I was always hugging and kissing them. Even to this day, I grab them both and kiss them on their heads when they least expect it. They don't pull away or fight me on it. They always see me kissing and hugging my little overweight Chihuahua. Lily was supposed to be a five-pound teacup but weighs in at ten pounds. I kid around and call her my "shorty two forty." Diane then scolds me and says that women don't like being called on their weight. The bottom line here is that my kids and my wife know that I love them. I have proven this to them time and time again. They know that I will never let them down and they can always count on me to be there for them. Even my overweight Chihuahua jumps into my arms when she is scared. That is very comforting for me because I didn't have that from Pat the Prick.

I knew two guys named George in my neighborhood. One lived across the street (George L.) and the other lived about a half mile away (George W.). Both were my age and went to the same local schools that I attended. Both of these Georges were tiny guys who needed to shoot their mouths off in order to be noticed. This was part of their personas. They were bullies who did outrageous things to people and acted tough. Both of them were constantly in trouble. I knew them very well and was never intimidated by these little pricks. We all got along when we hung out together. I have seen them in action and I was not impressed but their victims were scared of them. I never really saw them too much after I began high school since I did not go to the local high school.

Why did I dedicate one paragraph to these little bullies who I grew up with? The answer is simply because they had Napoleonic complexes just like my father. He was a little guy who grew up in the Bronx. He claims that he was a tough guy who always got in fights. The part that he stressed was that he always won those fights. I can't verify the stories that he used to tell and it is possible that he is just a legend in his own mind. I always took his stories with a grain of salt because I just didn't believe him.

I have established that George L., George W., and Pat D'Marco were all little bullies with Napoleonic complexes. They enjoyed bullying people and always shot their mouths off. Perhaps they thought that people would not notice them because of their stature issues. There is a common thread amongst these individuals that I needed to point out. These people can be characterized as aggressive bullies which is the most common type of bully. They think very highly of themselves, are strong and confident, and hot-tempered. In addition, they have trust issues and have little empathy for their victims. I can't speak for the two Georges that I knew in the neighborhood but I know that Pat came from a home where his father ruled with an iron fist. Many bullies are victims in their home environment and bullies outside of the home. It shouldn't be a surprise when I state that Pat ruled his home in the same fashion as his father. I do not fit the pattern of a bullying victim in any way. I was bullied at home but did not bully others. I don't claim to have been a choir boy but I only raised my fists to protect myself. I did not bully my family and my kids and wife are not intimidated by me. They certainly don't fear me.

When I look at the list of people who have been bullied by my father, I am amazed. He bullied his older brother until Phil died at fifty-nine years of age. Pat continues to bully Phil's three sons who are scared to talk to me for fear of reprisals from Uncle Pat. Pat bullied and controlled his mother for most of her life. He bullied me and my sisters as well as my mother. He even bullied his second wife. Out of all of the people who have been bullied by **Pat the Prick**, I am the only one who had the balls to push back. Eventually, I pushed back so hard that I eventually told him to fuck off in my own way.

When I discuss the subject of this book with friends, they are filled with disbelief. Perhaps they don't think that I would be a person who could have been bullied. I am a confident and intelligent person who at times can be quite intimidating. Like I said earlier, I don't fit the bill as a bullying victim. You can't always judge a book by its cover and that certainly applies to me. My family knows that I speak my mind and at times they are worried about what might come out of my mouth.

In 2010, I was testifying at a deposition (for the insurance carrier that I worked for) and I had linked a car accident fraud ring to the law firm that was deposing me. Midway through the deposition, the plaintiff attorney discontinued the proceeding because the links that I had established and testified about implicated them in a massive fraud. They told our attorney that they were scared of what would come out of my mouth next. At that point, they actually discontinued their lawsuit.

This type of intimidation has served me well over the years. I come across as a knowledgeable guy who you don't want to mess with. That is my persona and, despite appearances, people have pushed me around over the years. As they later find out, when I get my **Bronx Up**, they usually regret it. I don't just push back, I shove back (as my lovely wife has noted in the past). Diane knows who I am and if there is anything that she might not know about me, it is spelled out in detail in this book. She has benefited from my persona on multiple occasions and she knew what she was getting into when she married me many moons ago.

I am Son of Prick and I make no bones about it. I give people the benefit of the doubt until they give me a reason not to. The difference between me and Pat is that I choose to use my persona for good instead of evil. Bullying is evil and I am not a fan of any bullies. I am an honest guy and people know that but I guess human nature causes people to test me. People make the mistake of misinterpreting my kindness as a sign of weakness. I pick my battles in an effort to win the war. Pat has been on the receiving end of this test on multiple occasions and each time I have left him reeling. I always tell people that life is like a chess game. Each move deserves a counter move. As clear and concise as this statement is, I had an auditing supervisor who needed clarification. I issued that statement as a warning to her but she wasn't the sharpest tool in the shed and I was able to prove my point.

I never liked strategizing, but it is a necessary evil. When I put a plan into motion, I can anticipate what will happen next. I was performing a tax audit several years ago and a man who did not know me thought that he could bullshit me. He was one of those Wall Street guys who threw out a good line here and there. I saw right through his deception. I provided an "oh shit" moment for him by revealing something that I discovered during the audit. That important fact caused him to end the call and have his accountant call me less than one hour later. I made another revealing comment to the accountant and then he realized that the gig was up. Then they were willing to come to the table to negotiate on this audit and pay the back taxes that were owed.

Like I said earlier, I believe that life is like a chess game. Pat knew that I was good at chess as I always beat him when we played years ago. When I spoke to him last year, he said some things about my wife and then abruptly hung up the phone. It bothered me that I could not defend my wife, so I figured out a way to get the last word. My four-page letter spelled out many facts that were unpleasant, but truthful. If anyone saw my accusations then his perfect facade would be crushed. When I sent that letter, I knew what his response would be. It arrived two weeks later in the form of a "don't contact me ever again" letter. He couldn't even argue about any of the things that I wrote in that letter. Right on cue, he blew me off forever. I didn't just smack him in the face with the truth, I punched him in the gut over and over again.

I am **Son of Prick** and if Pat didn't know it, he knows it now. Once he receives his autographed copy of my book, the title will smack him in the face and remind him that I always get the last word. I will also thank him for providing the material that this book is based on.

Father Figure

Growing up in in a dysfunctional home in Whitestone, Queens was a way of life for me. It was all that I knew since we moved there in 1969 when I was only seven years old. Having a father who was a man lacking in character as well as empathy was also something that I didn't sign up for. Again, it was all that I knew.

Unlike many of my friends, I couldn't go to my old man for advice or help in any way. Pat was unable to sit down with his family and delve into a problem trying to seek a solution that suited everyone. In addition, he couldn't sit down with his family and enjoy them for who they were. He wasn't able to let his wife and kids be the people that they were supposed to be. We were subjected to his wrath non-stop for all of the years that we lived under his roof. Even after we moved out of his house, he tried to control us. Most of the time he was unsuccessful.

Kids are very perceptive and my kids were no different. As a seven-year old, my daughter told my wife and I something that shocked us to our core. She told us that Pat's second wife was a gold digger. Of course, we already knew that but our perceptive little girl pointed this fact out to us at such a young age. Not only did our little girl state the truth, but she played the song "Gold Digger" for us and we laughed our asses off.

My two children didn't have to worry about coming home to a dysfunctional home and the drama that this environment included. They had a tranquil house to come home to every day. My sisters and I didn't have that luxury. We would come home from school and watch the soap opera "General Hospital." We would be laughing and teasing each other as we relaxed after a long day at school. Then Pat would come home and we had to turn into the little busy bees that Pat expected. He couldn't accept that we were home relaxing and not doing anything useful. He would start barking orders and look for chores that he could find that would benefit his agenda.

My way to counter this madness was to avoid being home when the old man was home or on his way home. I had lots of friends and they welcomed me into their homes. I also had a lawn business that I started when I was thirteen years old. As such, I had the necessary excuses to be out and about. Any place was better than being home and subjected to Pat's work agenda and unnecessarily abusive environment. He was too stupid to see that his family used any excuse to get away from him. Avoidance was our best weapon in order to maintain our sanity. Unfortunately for us, we had to come home at some point and face the music.

When I was in elementary school, I learned something that I never knew. Kids my age that lived with their families did not fear their fathers and actually had good relationships with their parents. They didn't have to run away from their homes like my sisters and I did. They were not subjected to the ravings of a prick and clean freak who needed to get his money's worth from each of his family members. Our friends were able to embrace their parents and their homes. I was able to enjoy their family members and their homes as well. Not only did I have places to go but I had a reprieve from my tumultuous home life. People like the Milano's, the Perulo's, and the Berger's welcomed me into their homes with open arms. For that, I am forever grateful.

Tommy Milano Jr. was a young man who didn't have many friends during the period of time that he and I were close friends. We went to the same schools but were in different classes. We would hang out at his house in most cases. His father was a nice man and was so happy that his son had a companion. Tom Milano Sr. was doing well with his accounting and travel businesses and always took his family on elaborate vacations. He also bought his son the latest in photography equipment and everything else that his son wanted in life. He had the means to provide the best for his family. Tommy was perfectly content to stay inside his house and not do anything too exciting. I was always the one who wanted to go outside and run around or go bike riding. Tommy preferred to do things that he was used to doing by himself. One of the only times that we did go outside, we spent the afternoon using a magnifying glass to roast ants. I was always looking to do more. When the Milano's were fixing up their basement, Tommy and I were downstairs looking for something to do. I found pink insulation and before long I fastened a pink beard for myself. It was around Christmas time and I guess that I was getting into the Christmas mood. Before long, the two of us were walking around laughing and acting like Santa Claus. When it was time for me to go home, we both dropped our fake pink beards into the box that they came from. There was only one problem. The fiberglass particles were all over our faces. Mrs. Milano did her best to wash our faces to relieve our discomfort. She now had two seven-year old boys who were complaining and no matter what she did we didn't feel any better.

Tommy and I eventually spent less and less time together as we grew older. I was looking for excitement and adventure and Tommy doubled down on his photography and music. We basically grew apart. He wound up going to the Bronx High School of Science but he arrived there in sophomore year which was one year later than I began there. I would see him around and we would chat but our moments were too often very brief. I was having a blast in high school and Tommy was taking school much more seriously than I was. After we graduated from high school, I never saw him again. His family moved out of Whitestone and I moved to a neighboring area when my parents divorced.

The Milano's, Perulo's, and D'Marco's would all hang out together in the 1970s. We went away on vacation together and attended each other's parties. The Milano's had a boy and a girl. The Perulo's had two boys and my family had two girls and a boy. All of the kids were in the same age group and we had a lot of fun playing kick the can and swimming in the Perulo's built-in pool. Eventually, we all went our separate ways. Today, all of the kids are grown up and raising families of their own. My friend Tommy went on to become an E.R. physician and has his own practice in the New England area. I hope that he is doing well for himself.

Anyone reading this might wonder why I mention the Milano's at all. After all, this family doesn't further my memoir any further. I beg to differ. Tom Sr. was so kind and really spent a lot of time with his son. When I was at their home, he enjoyed spending time with both of us. He never once yelled at either one of us and was a very gentle man. When I saw the interaction that he had with his son, I realized that I didn't have that with my old man. At the age of seven years old, I realized that my father would never be like Mr. Milano. My father would never treat me as well as Mr. Milano treated his son. I understood at that tender age that I had at least one friend who was not beaten by his father. I was able to compare Tommy's household and family life to mine and the comparison was quite stark. I started wondering why Tommy wound up with a wonderful father and I didn't. I wasn't jealous, but it was a question that I started to think about from early on. Tommy loved his father and I hated mine. The father comparison was my version of polar opposites.

Steve Perulo had a wife and two sons. Teddy and I were always together and a lot of times we hung out with Teddy's twin brother, Henry. Henry was absolutely nuts. He would attempt things that were stupid and dangerous and would inflict bodily injury upon himself. My earliest recollection of his craziness took place when we were about eight years old. There was a swing set that was really big in the school yard of our elementary school. We all played in that school yard and I spent a lot of time on that swing set. Henry did also and he told Teddy and myself that he intended to swing so high that he would go over the top of the swing set. We told him that he was crazy and he did his best to reach his goal. He was reaching for the stars and one day, he actually did get the swing to fly over the horizontal pole on the top of the swing set. The problem was that he didn't know much about gravity. Gravity caused his body to come straight down and Henry hit the top of the swing set. I can't remember how many bones he broke on that fateful day, but he wound up in the hospital. Unfortunately for his parents, this was a common occurrence. When Mr. and Mrs. Perulo received a phone call from the school, they didn't have to ask which kid was in trouble or hurt. They rightfully assumed that Henry had done something and they had to bail him out.

I told Henry that if he wanted to kill himself, that I was okay with that. I asked him to do me a favor and not get anyone else killed in the process. He promised that he would think before he did anything else stupid. I was such a schmuck because I believed him. He dragged me and Teddy into the sewer system one day and we walked for miles underneath the streets of Queens. We knew that we could have drowned when the tide started to roll in but we were brave little explorers. When we entered the sewer system the water was about two inches high. We decided to turn around to exit the sewer when the water was up to our waists. We rushed to get out and made it out when the water was up to our armpits. We were lucky to survive that ordeal.

I didn't learn my lesson after we almost drowned in that disgusting, rat infested, sewer system. No, Teddy and I went back for more. The next stunt nearly cost us our lives also. Steve Perulo purchased a small sail boat that was twelve feet in length when we were teenagers. Our neighborhood was underneath the Throgs Neck Bridge. We would launch the boat in the park beneath the bridge. When we took this boat out, we were able to travel into the Bronx and sometimes we sailed in some treacherous waters. One day, the three of us were coming home from the Bronx. A tugboat was pushing several barges and probably didn't even see us. Henry steered us in front of the barges in an attempt to get across to the Queens' side. It was a stupid move as we yelled at him and told him to turn back. He said, "Don't worry, I got this." We pulled the sail closer to us in an effort to go faster. It was really windy and the top of the mast was inches above the water. Then, it happened. The top of the mast hit the waves which propelled the three of us off of the sailboat. The three of us were in the water and the sailboat was upside down. We were sitting ducks and death was bearing down on us. We were trying to get the sailboat moving again after we flipped it back over. Once the sail was extended and caught the wind, we were able to build up momentum and get moving again. All of this took place as these gigantic barges were bearing down on us. We managed to clear the barges and a police boat came over to check on us. They told us that we were really lucky to be alive. They had been watching us the entire time. Had the barges hit our sailboat, we would have been sucked under the barges and tug boat and the police would have been there to recover our bodies.

Henry reminds me of Tim (the Toolman) Taylor. Tim Allen had this great show which was really funny. Tim Allen's character would always get hurt and have to go to the hospital. The people in the E.R. knew him well and always had a cup of coffee and wheelchair ready for him. It was hilarious and it reminded me of my friend, Henry. Whether Henry was throwing M-80 fireworks (which again landed him in the hospital) or fracturing his spine on the diving board at Holy Cross High School, Henry was always getting hurt. Now we are in our 50s and we are all suffering from our old war wounds. I think that my old friend has too much to lose at this point. He has a wife and two children who are counting on him, so he is much more careful these days. I am glad because he needed to lose that crazy streak of his youth.

Steve Perulo was a rough guy just like my old man. I liked Steve who was a no-nonsense type of person. If his boys were out of line, he ruled with an iron fist. It shouldn't be a surprise that Steve and Pat were friends and worked for the same employer. I was always very respectful to Steve and his wife and I obeyed the rules of their house. Their house was a second home for me but if I did something stupid with his kids, Steve would reprimand me as well. He was a father figure to me as well and I certainly did enjoy spending time with the Perulo's. I only have fond memories of our time together in the old days.

The difference between Steve and Pat is that Steve was a good father and helped guide his boys into adulthood. He was there for his boys emotionally as well as physically. A perfect example of this was when Teddy had a bad day at work. Teddy was in his twenties at the time. He entered their house and Steve knew that something was troubling his son just by looking at his face. Without saying a word, Steve hugged his son and tried to help his son to resolve the problem. They talked about the issues involved and he supported his son through a very difficult period of time. Teddy told me this story recently and he felt very badly that I never had that kind of support. What Steve did that day for his son was a heartfelt gesture by a man who loved his kids and always supported his family. The love and support that he provided can never be taken for granted. In addition, Steve set an example for Teddy to follow as he raises his two children.

The Berger's lived two houses away from our home. Living on the same block with this family was really a blessing for me. Marvin and Eileen treated me like one of their own. It was comforting for me to have this family so close and they welcomed me into their home from day one. Jay and I were in the first grade together and we were classmates until our graduation at the conclusion of the sixth grade. We attended the same local junior high school and had a couple of classes together. Then I left to go to high school. Jay and I have been friends for the past fifty years. I ate over their house all the time. Mrs. Berger even made homemade chicken soup for me when I had a cold. She called it Jewish penicillin and it worked well for me. To this day, I enjoy chicken soup.

Jay and I would have sleep-overs at his house when we were younger and we always had a good time. Jay and his brother Michael were like the brothers that I never had. To this day, Jay can't believe things that I recall from our childhood. I recently reminded him about what Mrs. Oatley said to us in the fourth grade. Jay and I were chatting and Mrs. Oatley said, "Mr. D'Marco, MYOB. Is there anything that you would like to share with the class?" MYOB was her term for Mind Your Own Business. It was at that time that me and my good friend stopped chatting and began to pay attention to the teacher.

I worked for a company that made electronic signage while I attended St. John's University. Mr. Berger was an investor in that company and knew the owners very well. Mr. Berger had a successful law practice and was always ready to give me free legal advice. One day, I was over his house and he pulled me into his den so that we could speak. He wanted to give me fatherly advice. He said to me "I have known you since you were in elementary school. I am telling this to you because you are like one of my son's. Do yourself a favor and leave MTC and find another job. The owners of the company are driving it into the ground and when the dust settles, they will go bankrupt." He further explained that he was afraid that when this happened, he would be on the hook for some of the debts of the company. His instincts were certainly correct and the company did go bankrupt. He knew that the results were not going to be good and he wanted me to get out so that I didn't get stuck in the crossfire. His advice was given from the heart and I will always remember that. Here I was a twenty-three year old college graduate just embarking into the business world. I was not used to getting fatherly advice from anyone but I knew Mr. Berger since I was a seven year old child. I took this advice and ran with it. I applied for a position with an insurance company and was hired immediately. Over the years, Mr. Berger and I had many intense conversations about how insurance companies operate. We were on opposite sides of the personal injury automobile insurance equation. If I did have a case with his office, Mr. Berger would assign the case to one of his associates so that there was no conflict. I always had great respect for Mr. Berger and our relationship continues to this day. Sadly, his wife died recently. She was like a mother to me and was such a wonderful person. We all miss her to this day and think of her fondly.

No one was really comfortable at my house, this included my friends. Because of this situation, my friends would always invite me to come over to their residences. It worked well for me because I was always ready to hit the road and avoid the old man. Pat the Prick was always intimidating to anyone who came to our home and this made everyone uncomfortable. My sisters also didn't have much company because of the same reasons mentioned previously. I spent my early years running to other places every chance that I got. I needed to do this so that I could keep my sanity. My friends and their families loved it when I came over and they all treated me well. It didn't hurt that I was always respectful and polite. I have only fond memories of the Milano's, the Perulo's, and the Berger's. They all knew what I was up against. They knew my family and were able to see through the façade that Pat presented. Of course, they didn't know what went on behind closed doors, but these people were intelligent and were not fooled.

I never really had a fatherly influence on me in my youth. The situation with Mr. Berger was one of the only times that I can remember when someone was looking out for me because he cared about my well-being. Mr. Milano and Mr. Perulo also treated me well. I always appreciated the way that they treated me and perhaps they had an inkling about what it was like to live with Pat. They knew him well and spent much time with him over the years.

My father-in-law was another man who treated me like a son. Over the years, he gave me a lot of fatherly advice. He is gone now. He first met me when I was twenty-seven years old. I really enjoyed his company and he was more of a father to me than my father was. He was especially good to me after my open-heart procedures. He would pick me up and take me out to lunch all the time just to get me out of the house. During my six-month recovery, all of my in-laws were constantly helping us. They have never stopped helping us and being there for us. That is what a close family brings to the table and I want my kids to follow that lead so that we can all be close and help one another. I didn't have that growing up.

I wrote this chapter because I didn't have a real father when I was young and really needed fatherly advice and guidance. Instead, I was stuck with a man who treated me like an employee. He fed me and provided shelter. The necessities that he provided had a cost and I paid them back over and over again. I was a slave whose sole purpose was to work for the master. This man yelled at me, hit me, and basically treated me like shit. My father demanded respect because of who he was. I never gave it to him because he never earned it. He resented me because of this. He said that he saw the hatred in my eyes. I did hate him but I have to say that he did earn that hatred!

I grew up without a father figure who I could look up to on a daily basis. This created a void for me that I accepted. I knew that my kids needed a father who took care of them not because I had to but rather because they deserved to be loved and taken care of. I love my kids and providing love and guidance to them is something that I will always provide. My kids were never treated like employees. I provided fatherly advice for both kids because I wanted to and I did not want to repeat Pat's mistakes. If Diane and I ever become grandparents, those grandchildren will also get the same treatment from me. Not only do I want to be a good grandfather, I want to be the coolest grandfather in the world!

Life Goes On

There is a song that I enjoy listening to that refers to a son wondering if he will be the man that his father wanted him to be. The music video of this song really hammers home the fact that the singer really misses his father. This singer is sitting in front of his TV watching old movies of his father enjoying his son. The son now reminisces while drinking and pondering his future without his father being around.

This is not my life. I don't sit around drinking booze and watching old movies of the good old times. This is partly because I don't recall many good times with my old man. In my lifetime, I walked away from the old man three different times. I can apply some of Pat's twisted logic when I recall his words "three strikes and you're out." Well, this last stint is the longest at seven years and there will be no other opportunities for him. Years from now, I will not be appearing on some reality TV show seeing the old man for the first time in years.

Part of being a father involves being there for your children emotionally. Pat is devoid of emotion and I noticed this early on in my life. He never hugged me because I needed a hug or needed support. My conversations were limited to surface stuff because he didn't bring much to the table and any advice that he did provide was worthless. My mother had to step in and provide additional emotional support to make up for the inadequacies of her husband.

Pat was instrumental in who I became. This was not because he tried to teach me how to be a good person or to be a better father than he was. I was smart enough to learn from his inadequacies. My wife and I were there for our children physically and emotionally. Diane and I are empathetic and compassionate people and those around us can attest to this fact. We are reliable people who others can count on. I am lucky that I married a woman who I see eye to eye with most of the time and we are always on the same page. We believe in the team concept and we work out issues together. Pat was never interested in my mother's opinion because it was always his way or the highway. When relatives and friends have medical issues, Diane and I are always ready to assist them. When our kids have had medical issues, we spared no expense. We were there to make sure that everything went smoothly.

In 2008, Marisa had multiple surgeries to repair broken bones in her skull, the right frontal zygomatic area of her face, and her left ankle. As the nurses prepared her for her surgery, I was trying to comfort her. I promised her that everything would be okay. I also promised her that my face would be the last thing that she saw before the surgery and the first face that she would see when she woke up. With those words, a single tear ran down her face and she closed her eyes as the medications started to kick in. I gave her a kiss on her cheek and they wheeled her into the operating room. Since that surgery, my daughter has been in the hospital for other procedures. Diane and I have been there every step of the way.

Pat taught me how to ride a bicycle when I was about five years old. This is the only thing that Pat ever took the time to teach me. My Uncle Anthony taught me how to throw a baseball and football. Everything else I learned on my own or with the assistance of people who wanted to share things with me. I taught my kids how to ride bicycles in our neighborhood as I ran next to them to keep them from falling and getting hurt. We also played baseball, football, and basketball. When we installed a pool in our backyard, I was able to teach my kids how to swim. I spent a lot of time playing with my children over the years and I enjoyed every minute of it. People over the years have been very complimentary about our kids and I believe that Diane and I have done a great job in raising two well-adjusted children. I wouldn't do anything differently and our children are smart enough to see that they have had a nice, loving home to live in.

I was always an extremely nervous person. I walked around wondering what I was going to get in trouble for next. If I said the wrong thing or I accidentally broke something, Pat would make me pay. His punishment always came in the form of physical or verbal abuse. Most of the time he dished out my punishment with both types of abuse. I witnessed other family members receive the same type of abuse. It was constant and the norm in our home. As I completed high school, I knew that my mother had consulted with an attorney. She was under a lot of stress because she wanted to divorce Pat and I felt that stress as well. My breaking point came in the form of two peptic ulcers. I missed the last several weeks of high school due to this illness and the subsequent testing. I should have been enjoying time with my friends as we all prepared for our college years. Instead, I was home trying to recover from a very painful experience. My mother was also suffering with her colitis during this tense and forgettable period of time.

The day after my high school graduation party, Uncle Anthony showed up to drop the hammer on Pat. He totally caught my father by surprise and then he gave Pat the divorce paperwork. Pat swore up and down that he never touched Anthony's sister or Anthony's nieces and nephew. Of course, Pat was lying through his teeth. My father was scared of Anthony and for good reason. Anthony operated several illegal gambling stores and he was well-connected. Pat has small feet and didn't want to end up with cement boots!

Freedom was within reach for all of us. This family was always divided by **us verses him.** Whether he realized it or not, he was alone. Pat then pulled me aside and asked me if I wanted to live with him. He suggested that we could get a bachelor pad together. I practically laughed at him when I turned him down. I said to him "the way that you have treated me over the years and you expect me to live with you? I can't wait to get the fuck out of here. No, I will be living with my mother and sisters." With those words, I walked away from him.

Far be it for Pat to do the right thing. He refused to leave the house and we all lived together in a very uncomfortable situation. Pat even refused to let my mother sleep by herself. For several months, he slept in the same bed with my mother and this was intended to punish her. It was his form of emotional torture and when she couldn't take it anymore, she moved out of the house.

That summer turned out to be a very tense period of time for us. No one was speaking to him and he responded by being the biggest prick that he could be. He had a score to settle because of recent events. Then Pat decided to revisit a battle that he and I had been waging for years. He started yelling at me for not cutting the grass on the fifth day. This was an arbitrary number that he pulled out of his ass. My response was sudden and swift and he couldn't believe it when I told him, "cut your own fucking grass. I am out of here." With that, I moved out of the house. I didn't speak to him or even see him for over one year.

It was only with the urging of Grandma Nancy that I did eventually speak with Pat. I would visit with my grandmother in her apartment in Flushing. She was always good to me and I wanted to be a good grandson. Family actually meant something to me. When I review my past actions, I realize that I was justified in never meeting with Pat again. In hindsight, I should have avoided him like the plague and never looked back. I owed him nothing but I felt like I did. Just because he planted his seed doesn't mean that he deserved anything from me and he certainly never had my respect.

Respect is something that Pat's generation really thought was important. Being someone's father does not entitle you to respect. I believe that respect is earned. I have the respect of my children but that was not bestowed upon me because of a title. My kids respect me because of the way that I have treated them over the years. They respect me because I was there for them physically and emotionally. When they come to me with a problem, I tell them that "we never had a problem that we couldn't fix." I honestly believe that and I have convinced them that this is true. When the kids come to my wife and I for advice, we give it to them from the heart. We have no political motivations and no reason to give anything other than good and beneficial advice.

My kids are lucky that they have me and Diane for parents. My kids don't know dysfunction like I did growing up. They didn't have to listen to the screaming and fighting that was part of my life. My kids live in a home that is warm and loving and they were showered with love for their entire existences. I even comment that the dogs are lucky that they live here. Our three dogs enjoy their home as well. They have nice beds to sleep in and they eat well. They are well taken care of by the entire family. I have provided a glimpse into my home and the life that my family enjoys in this home. I was determined to provide a safe and non-dysfunctional home for my family and I think that my wife and I have succeeded in that sense. My kids love it here, maybe too much. They may never leave!

As calm and peaceful as things are here for all of us, I did notice something that occurred unexpectedly. As I grew older, my anxiety levels increased. The same thing happened to my wife and kids. Diane and I always had anxiety and it is certainly prevalent in both of our families. Our kids suffer with anxiety as well and I never saw that coming. Both of my kids are nervous individuals through no fault of their own. It was part of the DNA that they inherited from their parents. If I had told my father that I wanted to see a therapist, he would have smacked me in the head and told me to be a man and deal with it. Then he would have found some mindless job for me to do so that I didn't think about whatever was bothering me. Perhaps I could have waxed his car or the gutters!

I recently tried to talk with my three first cousins. I became very frustrated when none of them responded to my calls and emails. We always had a good relationship and the four of us would get together periodically to hang out. Then I spoke with my Aunt Ann Marie and she let the cat out of the bag. Pat basically warned everyone not to talk to me and my wife. It seems that my old man has once again bullied everyone into cutting all lines of communications with his son, the black sheep of the family. Aunt Ann Marie reminded me that "your father loves you." I did not want to give her any grief so I ended the call. I told my wife that "those are just words and they ring hollow in my mind." If Pat really loved me, would he try to isolate me from family members who I always got along with? In addition, my cousins are grown men who are my age and a little younger than I am. Not one of them tried to respond to me to give me a heads up. Instead, I feel like they were rude by not being responsive in any way.

This is who Pat is. This is his modus operandi. My family members were always very good at sweeping issues under the rug and never addressing them. Perhaps when Pat kicks the bucket, my cousins and I can re-connect. It is a shame since we all got along nicely and our kids are all in the same age group. I see some of my friends getting together with their family members and they schedule big picnics and get-togethers periodically. As long as Pat is in the mix, we will not be getting any invitations any time soon.

When Joanne passed away, I reached out to my father to express my condolences. Instead of having an intelligent conversation with me, he took the opportunity to complain about my wife. He basically took my wife's words, twisted them like a pretzel, and contorted them to fit his narrative. When I pushed back and disagreed with him, he hung up the phone.

I thought about what my options were and I decided that I would write a letter and send it to him. I had two themes that I wanted to address.

Life is Full of Choices – Pat was always afraid of being alone. He made his bed and now he has to lay in it. Now he was truly alone. He spent years making excuses about why he has three children and none of them speak with him. My letter debunked his excuses with the truth. I left no stone unturned and certainly did not hold anything back. I knew that when he read my words, he would turn them around on me and blame everyone but himself.

Life Goes On – Pat's three kids continue to live their lives and our families will continue to grow. He did not care what became of his kids and their kids so I sent some photos to document my points. I explained to him that Sally and myself had serious health issues. Donna recently got married, but she didn't want him to know about that union. I also wanted to inform him that his oldest grandchild, Nicholas, had a baby. This birth made Pat a great-grandfather so I congratulated him with his new title. Again, this is just a title that will never be earned.

Pat did receive my letter and photos. His response was typical for the prick that he is. He does not want to hear from me ever again "under any circumstances." This response was the one that I expected when I mailed my letter. It was my form of closure at the time. If that truth bomb hit him in the gut, I can only imagine what his response will be when he gets a copy of this book. This book is my work of art and it is truthful. My cousins and aunt will get autographed copies as well.

Aunt Ann Marie told me that there are three types of truths:

- My Truth
- His Truth
- The Truth

I have no reason to lie or twist the truth. I don't necessarily agree with my aunt's assessment. Pat always knew that I was bright and I made a living using my brain and my intelligence. He heard it from all of my teachers and other people who knew me. Perhaps he was jealous about the rave reviews that I received growing up. I don't think that he ever expected me to write a book and expose the fraud that he is.

I began this chapter by referring to the words of a song that I liked. Pat's response to my 1/22/2017 letter gave me the answer that I sought. His words were short and not so sweet when he wrote, "You are a devious bastard. You are a poor excuse of a man. I think you should get help from that Harvard educated pychiatrist. P.S. Do not under any circumstances contact me again."

My message to Pat was certainly not well received and I expected this type of response from him. The last time that I visited my psychiatrist, I told him that he was a pychiatrist instead of a psychiatrist and we both got a good chuckle out of Pat's words and this obvious misspelling. Pat believes that I am not the man that I was supposed to be. I am actually okay with these words because I am confident enough to know that Pat's opinion is only his opinion. My wife and kids do not agree with Pat's assessment. We all believe that this is why a certain ice cream manufacturer has thirty-two or thirty-three flavors. Like I said before, life goes on.

Living on Borrowed Time

When I am dead and buried, I want my family to be comforted by the fact that I left the world a better place than when I came into this world. There are a lot of people on this planet who live life by sucking all of the life out of everyone that they come in contact with. They are the takers, not the givers. I think of myself in the context of the latter.

Sam was my father-in-law. He died in 2007. We all miss him tremendously and it is hard to believe that he has been gone for more than a decade. I loved and respected him and I do not know of anyone who feels any differently about him. To this day, people tell us what a great guy that he was and they reflect on things that he did for them or said to them. He treated me just like a son and he certainly treated me more like one of his kids than my old man treated me. He was such a generous and giving man and we all aspire to be just like him.

I recall a perfect example of Sam's generosity and kindness. Diane and Sam were in the parking lot of a fast food restaurant when they saw a man taking food from a garbage pail. Sam gave Diane a twenty-dollar bill and told her to give it to this man. She did just that and the man went into the restaurant and bought food for himself. Sam didn't need any accolades, he just went and did what he had to do. He never tooted his own horn or told people what he had done. If Diane had not been with him that day, we would never be able to share this *act of kindness* story with anyone. He was a wonderful and religious man. I know that he watches over us and he is proud of what he sees.

I try to help people when I can. I have helped old ladies with groceries and have helped older people reach items that they couldn't reach on the top shelf in a supermarket aisle. Like Sam, I don't need accolades. All of those people that I have helped were grateful and thanked me for my good deeds. When I am dead and buried, I want people to remember me in a good light and say what a great guy I was as they reflect on some of the funny things that I have said or done. I want my kids to actually miss me and be upset when I do pass on. This will not be the case when my old man kicks the bucket. He spent his life taking from others and his world is shrinking before his eyes. Now that I have burned that bridge with him, I will not even know when he leaves this world. I can't honestly say that the world is a better place because of him.

I was born in 1962 and antibiotics were being used at the time. When I was five years old, I was diagnosed with rheumatic fever. I survived that serious health crisis because of the available medications and because of health professionals who were able to save my life. Had I been born fifty or even one hundred years earlier, I would have died during the fifth year of my life. The same can be said about another health crisis that took place when I was twenty-six years old. Bacteria from my mouth travelled to my heart after a dental visit and ravaged my mitral valve. The endocarditis was so severe that I eventually needed open-heart surgery to repair that damaged valve. I nearly died during those surgeries due to excessive bleeding, but again modern medicine came to my rescue. I thank God that I have intelligent and compassionate doctors like my cardiologist Dr. Martin Handler. He has been treating me for the past twenty-three years and I always tell people that he has been keeping me alive since 1995. I also tell people that my health situation requires that I have extraordinary doctors. I have used mediocre doctors in the past and those doctors could have left me six feet under.

It is for the above noted reasons that I feel that I am living on borrowed time. Every day that I wake up is a gift from God. Another gift from God was my son Joseph. If I would have died in 1997, during my second open-heart procedure, he would not be here. Diane and my little baby girl would have buried me. Diane would have moved on with her life. Perhaps there would have been another husband and additional children. **But** that did not happen.

Diane and I conceived another child who was born nearly two years after my surgeries. I honestly believe that God had a plan for me and Joseph was part of that plan.

That plan did not stop with conception. It began with conception and with every breath that I take the plan continues. I can no longer bring physical activities to the table but I can bring emotional and mental benefits to the table. I have used my time wisely with contributions to help mold and support my children. All of our difficulties have been confronted by a team concept and we have done our best to raise our children in meaningful ways. Diane and I are proud of our signature achievements. Our kids are running around trying to live their lives and establish themselves in this very complex world. I have no regrets and I make no apologies for things that I have done and said. I was not a mushy father who let people step all over me. Instead, I was a strong, confident, and compassionate man who believed in boundaries. It was not necessary to beat my wife, kids, and our little dogs. It was necessary to keep everyone in line but not with my fists and not by fear. I was determined to **not** be that kind of father. Pat did teach this lesson to me, but not by design. I was able to recognize that there are always better ways to do things and I continue to live my life this way.

The first time that Diane received a call from Marisa's high school informing us that Marisa cut school, we did not beat the crap out of her. That was never in the cards and never will be. When Joseph had school refusal, we did not throw him down two flights of stairs. We talked to our kids and tried to resolve those issues. When we couldn't handle the school refusal by ourselves, we hired mental health professionals. Whether or not our kids agree with our efforts, we wouldn't do anything differently. Our children are adults now and perhaps we have set a good example for them to follow. I wish our kids and their generation good luck because life was easier for our parents and therefore harder for our generation. I believe that the next generation will have their difficulties as well.

I have a lot more to give to this world. If I don't wake up tomorrow morning because it is time to go, I will be okay with that. I faced my mortality head-on and I appreciate any additional time that the Lord gives to me. There is more emotional support that I can provide to my wife and kids and I will continue to do so as needed. I see myself as a giver, not a taker. As generous as I believe that I am, my wife is much more of a giving person. My children were very lucky to have me and Diane as parents. We hope to enjoy grand-children and then we can continue to help them to be good people. We are also determined to avoid making the same mistakes that our parents have made over the years.

Should We Beat Our Children?

The $64,000 question is, should we beat our children or is there a better way to control our children? There is nothing more embarrassing than witnessing a totally out of control child. This is a child who has no respect for others and knows no boundaries. I have seen firsthand, children who are so spoiled that they do whatever they want and the parents are unable to control that child. Now multiply that by other siblings acting the same way and you are left with an outright *cluster fuck*. The parents in these types of situations look weak and pathetic. They are helpless to change the situation and the pattern continues and makes everyone involved embarrassed.

As a child, I remember my mother driving me and my two sisters out to Deer Park, Long Island. We didn't have car seats but the three of us sat in the back seat of our car. The three of us were fighting with each other and we were out of control. My mother couldn't wait to get to her cousin's home and she was panicking. She finally pulled over and told us that we were going to go home if we didn't behave. She threatened to tell our father and we all knew that if she did we would be on the receiving end of Pat's fist. None of us were willing to go down that road so we behaved better and Marie continued driving to Aunt Marge's home. We had a nice day and went home later that night. We all slept really well that night because six children spent the day running around in their backyard and playing in the woods. If Pat would have been in the car with us that day, we wouldn't have misbehaved at all. Kids always fight with one another but my sisters and I were petrified of our father. All he had to do was stare at us with "the look" and we knew that he meant business. It wouldn't matter where we were or who was looking. If Pat was pissed, he would hit us.

I was watching an elf give a speech to a bunch of little kids in Upstate New York when we visited a place called Christmas Town in the 1970s. I was sitting with about twenty kids and I was enjoying the show. The elf was interacting with this group of children and I asked a question. The elf replied to my question but as he was doing so, Pat smacked me in the head. I guess that Pat didn't appreciate my question and he wanted to let me know. Getting smacked in the head by Pat was a common thing for me. It was usually accompanied with a sick feeling in my stomach. It was the feeling of fear and a reminder that Pat was not finished. More reprisals might be on the way in the form of verbal or physical abuse. My sisters and mother also lived with this fear. Since Pat was such a bully, you never knew when he would strike next or who his next victim would be. I spent my life wondering what I would get in trouble for next. Sometimes I got in trouble for things that Pat perceived as being wrong. It was subjected to his interpretation which many times was just wrong.

Dinner time was a time when the entire family sat and ate together. My mother wanted us to act like a family and interact with each other. We would be talking and discussing how our school day went and Pat would be sitting there scrutinizing the conversation. If he objected to anything that was said, it stopped the conversation in its tracks. Many dinner conversations were sabotaged by this moody man. If he was pissed, he would slam his fist on the table and declare that he was the **patron**. This was a term that I had never known about but Pat interpreted it to mean that he was the boss. He told us that it was an Italian term and the dictionary indicates that it was an ancient Roman term. It refers to a person who frees a slave but retains the rights over that slave. That just about sums up our existence in his home because we were all his slaves. We were all subjected to his twisted views and extreme logic and if you ever questioned him about anything, you would certainly be made to regret it.

Fear and intimidation were part of the *Pat Plan.* The moment that you veered from his program, you were subjected to Pat's wrath. We all lived in constant fear of this man and worried what bug would be up his ass when he came home. As soon as Pat walked in the door, all of our demeanors changed because we knew that the party was over. He would start barking orders at all of us. He would say to my sisters, "What are we having for dinner?" He would look at me and say "Why isn't the lawn cut? Why aren't the garbage pails out at the curb?" When my mother came home from work, he would get on her for something. If he was mad at someone, and he usually was, he would start bitching at that person. This constant state of fear caused so many health issues for all of us. The one person who didn't suffer was Pat. Besides being a prick, he was a healthy prick who was never sick in his entire life.

I recently asked my daughter if she was ever afraid when she knew that I was coming home. She replied that she was never scared of me at all. When we owned part of a laundromat, I would go there at night and review the daily proceeds. Marisa would call me and cry for me to come home because she wanted to play. That would make me finish up my chores quicker because I couldn't let my little girl down. Joseph was younger than Marisa and we always included him in our playtime festivities. I loved entertaining my kids and spending time with them because I never had that as a child. I didn't want my kids to fear me like I feared my old man. I needed to be there physically and mentally for my kids.

When my children were young, we lived across the street from an elementary school. Directly across the street was a baseball diamond. It was on that field that I played with both of my kids. We played baseball, threw around a frisbee, went on the swing sets, rode bicycles, rode skateboards, and ran around and chased one another. I remember when my mother-in-law bought Marisa a pink motorized car. I would follow Marisa as she rode it around the base paths of the baseball diamond. A big cloud of dust would be trailing this pink plastic battery-powered car. Then my wife would have to get Marisa in the bathtub so that she could wash out the dust that was in Marisa's hair.

My kids were really good kids. We did spank them once in a while, but it was rare. I remember telling Marisa that "if you do that again, I will spank you so hard that your brother will cry." Of course, I was joking but my kids thought I was serious! There was no reason to beat my kids. I loved them so much, hitting them would only make them fear me. That fear would eventually turn to hatred and my relationship with them would be shattered. I was not willing to go down this road like my old man did. My sisters and I were not bad kids. Did we get into trouble here and there? Yes we did, but it was such minor stuff. All kids get into some type of mischief.

Pat claimed that he was a good father because none of his kids "got arrested or got knocked up." I set the bar higher for myself and I believe that I was a good father because I loved my kids and helped guide them into adulthood by being there physically, emotionally, and mentally. The barometer that I use is that my kids love me and they know that I would do anything for them. My children are adults now and they are both wonderful and respectful human beings who are giving and helpful to others. They are not here to suck the life out of anyone and this world is a better place because of them. They are givers, not takers.

Were my kids always angels? No, but I found a way to keep them in line. Instead of using my fists, I used my brain. I invented a story line about a mean old lady. Mrs. Keen really did live behind our home. The back of her home could be seen from our backyard. Both backyards butted against each other. I met Mrs. Keen and she was such a bitch. She and I had words when Diane was pregnant with Marisa. She yelled at me when she saw the fence that I built to separate our backyards. She didn't like my beautiful cedar fence that I built from scratch. She told me to remove it and when I refused she told me that her lawyer would make me take it down. I told her to "bring it on." That was my only contact with this ornery and unpleasant woman. The fence is still standing and we have since moved to another part of town.

When Marisa was about five years old, she was giving me a hard time about something. I told her that "if you don't cut it out, I will send you to Mrs. Keen's house until you learn your lesson." I explained that other parents in the neighborhood send their kids to Mrs. Keen and she straightens out the kids. When they are better behaved, they get to come back home. I made Marisa look out of her bedroom window and I showed her which bedroom she would be living in. I also explained that she would not get dessert at night, as Mrs. Keen didn't like ice cream. I would have to pay Mrs. Keen for her services but it would be worth it if she did her job for us. I compared Mrs. Keen to the Wicked Witch of the West. I painted such a vivid picture of Mrs. Keen, that Marisa was petrified of a woman who she had never met. When Joseph was old enough to understand, I showed him the window of the bedroom that they would be living in. Both of my kids feared this woman. One morning when Marisa was behaving badly, Diane let Marisa speak with Mrs. Keen on the phone. In reality, it was my mother-in-law on the phone. Grandma Camille changed her voice and sounded like a really mean woman. Marisa got off the phone and was such a good girl after speaking with the meanest old woman in the neighborhood.

One day, Diane and I decided to take our kids out east. We travelled to Greenport and spent the day there. The kids went on the carousel and then we ate in a nice restaurant before heading back home. Both of our children were strapped into their car seats in the back seat of our van. They were hitting each other during the trip home and no matter what we said to them, they both continued to fight with one another. I warned them that I would drop both of them off at Mrs. Keen's house if they didn't stop fighting. When we reached our neighborhood, I stopped at Mrs. Keen's home. I opened the van door and rang Mrs. Keen's doorbell. I knew that Mrs. Keen was in Florida. She is what we call a "snowbird" because she could afford to spend the winter in a warmer climate. I looked at the horrified faces of my children when I told them to get out of the van. I told them that Mrs. Keen agreed to take both of them and I would drop off their clothes and toothbrushes later that night. Both kids were crying and Marisa said, "No Daddy, we promise that we'll be good. We don't like Mrs. Keen." They both swore that they would behave and then we went home. I was laughing inside, but I felt badly that I made them cry. Once home, Diane and I gave each other a high-five for a job well done.

Did Diane and I get a lot of mileage out of the Mrs. Keen threat? Absolutely and I make no apologies for telling this white lie. I achieved the results that I was looking for. I was smart enough to outsmart my kids by being creative. I laugh because Marisa babysits for our nephew and some other kids in the area. She uses the Mrs. Keen threat and our nephew doesn't like Mrs. Keen either. We all pile on the bullshit when using that threat and it works especially well. I anticipate getting more mileage out of this fictional character in the future.

When I was a kid, my father beat the crap out of me more times than I care to remember. It was common for me and my sisters to get hit if any of us were out of line. Today, if you hit your kids, you can have serious legal problems. Social services will be looking to take your kids away from you. That would just make a messed-up situation even worse. By using the Mrs. Keen threat, we were able to keep our kids in line. It made our kids know some type of fear and it worked for us. This is the answer to my $64,000 question and if I had to do it over again, I wouldn't change a thing.

I don't toot my own horn when it comes to child-rearing. I did the best that I could. Diane is mostly responsible for raising our children. She was the stay-at-home mom who took care of her children. She nursed them as infants and she used her medical skills to make sure that the children were in good health and stayed that way. She was an excellent mother and our children are the results of her efforts. If she was a lousy mother, then Marisa wouldn't be telling us that she wants us to help her raise her children in the future.

Marisa recently told Diane, "Dad is home all day and doesn't do anything. He can babysit my kids when I have them. I will drop off Savanna (her pit bull) and the kids and he can take care of them." All I can say is, that I am so happy that my lovely daughter is planning my future as well as hers! I guess that my thirty-two years in business and my two college degrees make me a great candidate to be subservient to my daughter and all of her whims! I am glad that she trusts me but you would think that her insensitive comments were coming from someone who was born and raised in the Bronx. I was born in the Bronx, not Marisa. This comment makes it clear that my daughter does not fear me and trusts me enough to raise her children. She may not remember the time that I actually changed my son's diaper. I thought that I did a good job. We were in a clothing store afterwards and Joseph's diaper and his shorts dropped to the floor. His manhood was exposed until my wife grabbed our child and fixed the mess that I had made!

If I were a bully and my kids did not appreciate the way that I treated them over the years, they both would have moved out of our home when they turned eighteen. That is what I did. Diane and I provided a loving home for everyone and we didn't bully anyone. There is no dysfunction here and I feel like I met the goals that I set years ago. My kids are safe here and this is a sanctuary that we maintain. I always say, "This is my castle and I come here to keep the world out." Our home is a **No Bully Zone** and that will never change.

The D'Marco Kids

What is the best way to handle a bully? Should you run away from them and cower in the corner? Should you do your best to fight back and send a message that you will not take their shit? There are no easy answers and people have been grappling with these types of issues since the beginning of time.

My daughter, Marisa Grace, was always a really cute kid. She was always compliant and respectful to everyone. A doctor once told us that "she has some temper." That doctor was correct because when Marisa gets pissed off enough, she is willing to shove back. At times, she can be quite the bitch.

We decided to send our daughter to a local catholic elementary school. A bus would stop on the corner across the street from our home every day. We would let Marisa get on the bus and we were comforted by the fact that she would be safe in the care and custody of the bus company and the school. We relied on this assumption and yet both of our kids were bullied at this catholic school. The school was run by a nun and another woman. We complained and asked for help in dealing with the bullying issues that involved our son. Both administrators demonstrated how inept they were in dealing with these situations that we brought to their attention. In my estimation, both were the **useful idiots** who were only interested in taking care of the wealthy and powerful families in the area. We were not part of that crowd.

Lisa Mooney was another child who took the same bus that stopped on our corner. She lived several blocks away and was much older than Marisa.

When Marisa was in the first grade, Lisa was in the eighth grade. Lisa would bully our daughter and take her lunch money. This went on for about one week and Marisa told Diane that someone was bothering her. Diane offered to help but Marisa said that she would take care of it herself. Marisa had a big surprise for Lisa Mooney at the beginning of the next week. Lisa demanded that Marisa hand over her lunch money. Instead of getting money, Lisa Mooney received a punch in the mouth! This one act by my little girl solved her problem immediately. Lisa Mooney never bothered Marisa ever again. I guess that Lisa was not fond of the *knuckle sandwich* that Marisa served on that particular day.

Years later, we threw a party for Marisa's Sixteenth Birthday. We chose to use the Knights of Columbus Hall which is located in our neighborhood. We had more than one hundred people at this party. Some of the kids showed up drunk and made messes in the bathrooms. We did not provide any alcohol at this party and I was tasked with calling the parents of the kids involved. Marisa came up to me at the beginning of the party and pointed out that one of the employees was Lisa Mooney. She was pouring soda at the bar and she looked very uncomfortable for the entire night.

I wish that I could say that Marisa's experience in the first grade was the only time that she had to deal with bullies. Other kids in the school bullied her when she was in the upper grades. One of their favorite tactics was throwing pennies at her during lunch. We didn't live in the ritzy part of town like those kids. We chose to live in the neighboring area. The ironic thing about those kids who were throwing pennies at my daughter is that Marisa probably had more money in her bank than they did.

Joseph is nearly four years younger than Marisa. We felt good that Joseph's older sister was with him to keep an eye on him during the school day. She always loved her baby brother and she would always protect him. The early years in that school were uneventful. When Marisa graduated and went to a different school, all hell broke loose for our son. When Joseph was in the sixth grade, there were about nine kids in that grade who started bullying him. The ring leader was a kid named William Holtz. The surprising thing about this kid is that he is a little shrimp and comes from a very dysfunctional home. His parents adopted him and the father was a local businessman. Mrs. Holtz was the town drunk. People had complained that Mrs. Holtz had driven their children around town and she was drunk. The school administrators knew about this family's secret but since Mrs. Holtz was on the school's board of directors, they were willing to ignore the problems in the Holtz home.

Our problems started when we dropped our son off at the Holtz's home. Several hours later, Mr. Holtz unexpectedly showed up at our home with our son. He had been bitten in the face and arm by their dog. Apparently, Mrs. Holtz was too drunk to deal with the situation so her husband had to deal with the problem. Diane cleaned Joseph's wounds and they healed beautifully. Joseph received additional invitations to the Holtz home after that incident but we would not let him go there. William Holtz and his cohorts decided that our refusal to let our son hang out in an unsupervised setting was a noteworthy offense. If Mrs. Holtz was drunk, then she couldn't properly supervise twelve-year old boys. We didn't want history to repeat itself. This set the whole scenario in motion.

Joseph would get nasty phone calls on his cell phone so he would block all of their numbers. Then they would interrupt his X-box games when he was playing with other friends. He would block them from his games and they would contact his other friends. These bullies would connect with Joseph's other friends and then they could get back into Joseph's computer and headset. Then, they tormented Joseph in school and the inept administrators wouldn't do anything about it. I was pissed off because I coached many of those kids when I was one of the basketball coaches and I knew many of the kids and their parents. William Holtz also spent a lot of time at my home and in our pool. We were very good to that boy and felt bad about his home situation. His way of thanking us was certainly different than what I expected.

I always believed that *Papa Bear* needed to protect his cubs. I jumped into action by contacting my cousin who was a local cop. He provided me with the phone number for the detective squad. Before I followed up with those detectives, I reached out to the school. I spoke to the "unholy nun" who was more interested in protecting the nine boys involved than protecting my son. She made it clear to me that there was nothing that she could do. She was more worried about the tuition revenue that these nine kids provided than the revenue that we provided for the previous six years. In addition, some of the parents were politically connected and she couldn't piss off those parents. As a kid I always said, "money talks, bullshit walks." Well, here was my proof. We paid $2,500.00 annually for Joseph's tuition but those nine kids paid $22,500.00. The nun made a business decision instead of making the right decision.

This nun did not heed my warning about those bullies. The next year, these nine boys hurt another boy. They distracted the lunch lady and lifted up their victim. They spread his legs and rammed his scrotum into a pole. He wound up having to get medical attention and there is the possibility that he will not be able to have children. Again, this nun protected those nine boys who were really malicious. They say that "karma is a bitch" and someday these bullies will find out how true that statement is. Those nine kids are not good people and they will grow into adulthood as bullies. This is especially true if their devious actions never have any real consequences. Those school administrators swept the problem under the rug instead of taking a stand and trying to fix the problem. Joseph said to me once that "William is living in his own personal hell" and he does not harbor any resentment against that boy.

Joseph left that catholic school and went into the local public school at the beginning of the eighth grade. He never looked back and he is moving on with his life. This is one of those life-changing events that can forever shape someone. He did tell me that I did the wrong thing when I called William's father and threatened him with the detective squad. Following that call, Mr. Holtz made William apologize for his actions, but the bullying never stopped.

This is the world that we live in today. If someone wanted to bully me in the old days, they would have to be in my face in order to do it. Today, the technology is so advanced that people can bully others using technology and they hide behind it. This is the coward's way of being a bully. William Holtz is the poster child for this statement. My son is at least half a foot taller than William. In addition, Joseph is a strong young man. Joseph could have physically beaten the crap out of this bully and yet he never did. Like I said earlier, many bullies are cowards.

The Philly Connection

Grandma Nancy D'Marco had two children. Philip was her oldest son and Pat was about four years younger. As the youngest child, Pat was spoiled by his mother. Grandpa Joe was a boxer in his younger days. He had steel blue eyes and a wide nose from making a living in the boxing ring. When he could no longer support his family as a fighter in the Bronx, he worked as a security guard. Grandpa Joe worked security at night and he slept during the day. When his sons were home, they would fight with each other and disrupt their father's sleep. He would wake up and discipline his boys with his fists. As Phil and Pat grew older, their issues with each other would intensify. Grandpa Joe found a solution that was very patriotic. Both boys would go into the military upon completion of high school. Phil went into the army and became a tank commander. When he completed his enlistment, he returned to the Bronx and became a New York City firefighter. Pat enlisted in the navy and wound up on a ship that performed maintenance on other ships. To this day, Pat struggles with nausea whenever he goes out on the water.

To say that Phil and Pat had many issues in their relationship is an understatement. They had rivalries going back many years and their differences were never resolved. Phil had a wife and three boys and Pat had a wife and three children. Whenever the two families got together, the family issues surfaced. I remember years going by and not seeing my cousins. Other times, I remember seeing them a lot.

Phil owned a small boat and we would go out for daily fishing trips during the summer. One day, when my cousin Danny and I were in elementary school, we were fishing on the front of the boat. The anchor was down and we were sitting on an area that was part of the boat but not meant for sitting. Another boat came racing past us and Uncle Phil started yelling at them to slow down. The wake from their boat caused our boat to rise and then dip. With that dip, Danny and I slid into the bay. I can recall Uncle Phil pulling me into the boat by lifting me using my belt. Pat grabbed Danny and pulled him into the boat. After that incident, we weren't allowed to sit in the front. I really enjoyed fishing with Danny and his younger brother Anthony. Phil and Pat enjoyed taking us out on the boat. The best thing that I ever caught was a pillow and it had a crab on it. We did catch local fish but we mostly caught sea robins, which are not edible. We would catch them and then throw them back into the water.

When we went fishing, we would eat our sandwiches and drink cans of soda. Then, when we had to relieve ourselves, we dropped our shorts and peed into the water. This tiny boat did not have a bathroom so we did what we had to do. One day, Pat decided to make my life miserable. I was trying to relieve myself and he rocked the boat so violently that I nearly fell into the water. He was being such an asshole that I never relieved myself. I held it in until we arrived at the dock and Danny and I ran to the bathroom. None of us thought that Pat was funny and he was the only one laughing.

Uncle Phil and Aunt Lidia had a home in Babylon, Long Island. I spent a lot of time at their house. Danny, Anthony, and myself would ride bicycles throughout their neighborhood. One day when I was about seven years old, we stopped at a local convenience store for a soda. A couple of older boys started pushing me and Danny around and were bullying us. We didn't notice that Anthony slipped away and he told his father what was going on. Uncle Phil showed up at the scene and caught these kids smacking us around. Uncle Phil grabbed these kids and pushed them away as he yelled at them. Those boys ran away as fast as they could and Uncle Phil followed us back to his house.

I always enjoyed Uncle Phil's company and I certainly enjoyed it way more than spending time with my old man. Uncle Phil was always nice to me and he was fun to be with. He would always tell me these corny jokes that he learned at the fire house. At times, I wished that he was my father instead of Pat. Everyone enjoyed spending time with Phil. He died suddenly, at the age of fifty-nine and this shocked all of us. His boys and their wives were really heartbroken when he passed away. Brianna was his oldest grandchild and she really took his passing badly despite her young age. I never heard anyone say anything bad about Uncle Phil and I only have fond memories of him.

When I turned thirteen, Uncle Phil would take us deer hunting. I didn't have a rifle but he would provide one for me whenever we went. Uncle Phil took the time to educate me about hunting and he taught me how to hunt. He enjoyed sharing his knowledge with me and he would take me to the shooting range and help me practice my shooting skills. When I had my own car, I would meet Uncle Phil and his sons by their house. Uncle Phil gave me good advice when he helped me pick out my 30-06 rifle and also my compound bow. Then he showed me how to use them and I appreciated him taking the time to help me. He knew that I was a good kid and I was his godson. Every year, I would go hunting with Uncle Phil and his three sons. Pat came with us some of the time. We would camp in the woods and really rough it when we hunted. Uncle Phil would cook for us and we would have a blast together. We spent good quality time together without the distractions of TV, electronics, and the other parts of city life.

When I look back on our hunting trips, I recall one thing that always disturbed me. I never liked the way that my father treated his brother. Pat would talk to Phil as if he was a piece of shit. Pat had no qualms about making fun of his brother in front of Phil's kids. No one ever said anything to Pat and it was a constant thing every time that we got together to hunt or fish. Pat probably always bullied his older brother. It would make sense that when Pat and Phil were kids, they would always fight because of Pat's bullying. I only know what I saw when I was a teenager. Phil would just accept the bullying and never fight back. It probably was always a way of life for him. When I reflect back on those hunting trips, we always had more fun when Pat wasn't around. Pat just brought chaos to the mix and Uncle Phil and I were able to relax when Pat was absent.

I can still remember many of Pat's comments that were directed towards Phil:

- "stop smoking, the deer will smell you,"
- "you're so fat, you can't walk far to get a better spot,"
- "keep eating like that and you will wind up dead like Dad,"
- "turn the heat up, you cheap fuck,"
- "this food tastes like dog food,"
- "you're so stupid."

I once told one of my brothers-in-law to "grow a pair of balls." I apologized to him afterwards because it was a comment that was over the top. I also apologized because I said it in front of one of his kids. Pat always bullied his brother in front of his kids. My three cousins never said one thing about the comments that Pat made to their father. It bothered me at the time and made me very uncomfortable. I can only imagine how they felt. I know how Uncle Phil felt because I was on the receiving end of comments like the ones that I described. Uncle Phil's facial expressions told me that he did not appreciate the bullying. It must have bothered him that those comments were made in front of his kids. When I reflect back on those types of issues, it makes sense that there was friction between the brothers. Phil must have been subjected to this abuse for his entire life.

The bullying continues to this day even though Phil has been gone for a very long time. My cousins are too scared to talk to me to this day. Pat told them to ignore me and they would not want to piss off Uncle Pat. My cousin Steven is the youngest of Phil's three kids. Steven married Jeannine many years ago and Diane and I were not invited to the festivities. Pat and I were not speaking at the time. Pat promised that he would make it up to Steven financially so Steven obliged Uncle Pat. Years later, Pat actually admitted to me that he asked Steven to exclude me from that wedding. My cousins and I discussed this issue years ago and it seems that history is certainly repeating itself. Pat was always a bully and will never break out of that habit.

Terry Murray

In 1974, I graduated from P.S. 193 Alfred J. Kennedy Elementary School in Whitestone, Queens. I then attended the seventh grade at P.S. 194 William Carr Junior High School which was also located in Whitestone, Queens. I completed the seventh and eighth grades at this school before entering the Bronx High School of Science in 1976. Many of my former classmates also attended P.S. 194 as well. Jay Berger was also in many of my classes. I remember some of the older students calling me "Blue Boy" because I always wore blue jeans, blue tee shirts and sometimes a blue hat. That name was not such a big deal and it didn't bother me at all.

I enjoyed my new surroundings and I was meeting kids from other parts of Queens. This school was larger than the elementary school and there were more students in this school. In P.S. 193, I spent grades one through six in the IGC Program with the same group of twenty-five kids. In this junior high school, there were different kids in each class and when the bell sounded we went to the next class with different people. It was here that I started to notice some of the girls and began to be interested in some of them.

I met Terry Murray in the seventh grade. He lived in Whitestone with his family. I went to his house once and his family members were very nice to me. We threw a football around and maybe even a frisbee. We didn't hang out very often. He was a skinny kid with buck teeth and greasy hair. He dressed just like I did with jeans and tee shirts. He was in my math class with Mrs. Green in the seventh grade.

Mrs. Green was an elderly lady but she didn't maintain control of her classroom very well. I sat in the back of the classroom with a bunch of boys who could not sit still. I remember that there was a square desk that was bolted to the floor and one of my classmates started tugging at the desk and it started to come apart. When the teacher was writing on the blackboard and could not see what was going on, we were ripping this desk apart. It made a lot of noise when it was getting ripped apart and the teacher would turn around to see what the noise was but she continued to write on the blackboard. What do you do with the broken wooden pieces of a desk when you destroy it? One of us had the brilliant idea of throwing it out of the window. Piece by piece, it went sailing out of the window until the whole desk was outside on the front lawn. Our classroom was on the second floor. The principal's office was directly below our classroom. When the principal was looking out of his window, he saw this wood landing outside on the lawn. He came up to our classroom and was asking questions and looking around. The teacher was totally oblivious to what was going on. None of us got in trouble that day.

My only other encounter with the principal took place at the end of the eighth grade when several of my friends and I were caught cutting out of graduation rehearsals. We probably made it easy for him. We left the auditorium and walked passed the front lawn where the principal's office was. He came running out the building and caught up with us. He threatened to prevent us from graduating but he went easy on us and we did graduate on graduation day.

The mailman in our neighborhood knew all of the kids on the block. He would come to our house and our dog would try to bite him. All dogs hated the mailman so Lady was no different. Our mailman would use a leather strap to hold the mail together. He would leave these straps on our mailboxes and I would use mine to carry my books to school. I was not the only person receiving these leather straps. Other kids in the school had these straps as well. What would junior high school kids in Mrs. Green's classroom use a leather strap for? Terry Murray could answer that question very easily. He would be taking notes and paying attention to the teacher and he would be getting whipped with these straps. The straps had a metal clasp on the end and that was the part that the bullies were hitting this defenseless kid with. They were trying to inflict pain on this boy for no apparent reason. It was like a group effort by these bullies. The teacher would be writing on the blackboard and Terry Murray would be getting hit in the back, neck, and all over by these kids. He would be crying out in pain and the teacher would continue with her lesson. These bullies would also knock Terry's books on the floor and when he went to retrieve them, they kicked him and hit him with the leather straps again. They would take his pen and throw it across the room. I never once hurt him in any way but I am sorry that I did not try to help him. I guess that I didn't want to be on their shit list like he was.

The bullies in this school were relentless. I remember walking in the halls with Terry when the bell rang. We were switching classes and someone knocked his books on the floor. He bent over to pick up his books and someone kicked him. Other kids kicked his books down the hallway. When he tried to pick up the books, he was knocked to the ground. This didn't happen only one time. It was constant. I really felt badly for him. The extent of my assistance was to help him retrieve his books but I never stood up for him and I never prevented any of the abuse that he suffered through.

When it came to Terry Murray, it seemed that all of the bullies were on the same team. This poor kid couldn't walk down the hallway without getting spit on, kicked, or hit with the leather straps. It was as if he had done something terrible and they hated him for it. I knew him and he was just like the rest of us. He was trying to fit in and they would not let him. We were also going through puberty which meant that we had those teenage hormones flowing. In addition to all of this, the boys were showing off because the girls were blossoming right before our eyes. Once I graduated from junior high school, I never saw Terry Murray again. I hope that he recovered from all of the bullying that he endured and is living a good life. He deserves that much. I was physically abused by my father at home and I didn't want to get into the line of fire at school. I am sure that everyone knew a "Terry Murray" at their school.

I realize that sometimes people set themselves up to be bullied. Terry was one of those people. He came to school with dirty clothes and greasy hair. One student even taped a sign on his back without his knowledge. The sign said "kick me" and believe me, there was no shortage of kids willing to oblige that sign. He was walking down the hallway and he couldn't understand why people were picking on him more than usual. Eventually, I realized what the problem was and I pulled the sign off his back. When I handed this paper sign to him, it all made sense. Mrs. Green had a box of tissues on her desk in case some of her students needed to blow their noses. One day, Terry needed a tissue but he did not go to her desk to grab one. She made an example out of him on this particular day. She singled him out by saying to the entire class "Terry, when we need to blow our nose, we don't wipe our nose with our shirt sleeves." Then she proceeded to demonstrate what he had done. I felt so bad for him. Even this elderly teacher was embarrassing this young man by ridiculing him in the middle of a math lesson.

In the seventh grade, I was trying to get acclimated to this new school. Then I witnessed the results of a female bully really destroying her victim. The victim was beaten up so badly after school. It was such a lopsided fight because the bully destroyed this other girl. The victim was getting punched in her breasts, genital area, and face so badly. One of the teachers broke up the fight but not until the victim was totally decimated.

My early schooling was spent in the public school system in New York City. My mother attended a catholic school in Harlem when she was young. She was bullied very badly by a teacher at this one school. The catholic nuns had a reputation for being tough on the students and my mother was victimized by one vengeful nun. My mother has a medical condition called colitis which is an intestinal inflammation that has plagued her throughout her entire life. She would miss a lot of school due to this issue and when the nun picked on her, it only extended her absences and made her medical issues worse. This nun didn't understand or didn't care until my grandmother went to the school to discuss the situation with the principal. Shortly thereafter, my mother attended a public school in the Bronx and completed her education.

If we talk to our parents who went to school years ago, I am sure that they will have stories to tell that involved people being bullied. As a kid, I used to watch **"Little House on the Prairie."** This was a television series that took

place in a fictitious town in the Midwest during the 1800s. It showed how difficult life was for the people who tried to start new lives as farmers and mer-
chants during the westward expansion into the new territories. There were a
bunch of bullies in that show and the bullies were both boys and girls as well
as adults. The stories that were highlighted in that show were fictitious but
perhaps there was some truth to the stories that they were telling. My only
point is that bullying has been going on for thousands of years and it will continue for millennia and even after we are all gone.

Robert Paster – The Scariest Bully Ever

Sophie was one of our neighbors when we bought our first home in 1992. Over the years, we have spent a lot of time with Sophie and her family. Sophie has one child and thought that her body would never be able to carry a pregnancy to full term due to medical issues. Sophie and Diane were speaking about Sophie's miscarriages one day at our home. Diane has expertise about such issues since she spent her career working as a registered nurse in the OB/GYN and Pediatric fields. Diane floated the possibility of adoption with Sophie and her response was quite different than Diane expected. She said to my wife, "when you adopt a child, you are getting someone else's problems."

Thankfully, Sophie's opinion is not the norm. Adoption is a wonderful alternative for people who cannot conceive children on their own. For every horror story that you may hear about, there are an abundance of stories that are positive. I have an aunt who was adopted and she is a beautiful person and her family is wonderful as well. Diane's paternal grandfather was adopted as an infant and was loved by everyone in the family. My father-in-law loved his father and my wife really enjoyed spending time with her grandfather. He was a musician and conductor who played the violin at Carnegie Hall in New York City. Unfortunately, he died in 1972 when Diane was only seven years old. Grandpa Tony had four grandchildren and since Diane was the oldest, she knew him the best. The other grandchildren either don't remember him or barely remember him. Diane remembers going places with Grandpa Tony and he always had a can of sourballs in his car. He was always thrilled to take Diane with him and he enjoyed feeding her sweets. Diane was also the one grandchild who inherited his musical abilities. His piano currently sits in our living room and my wife plays it beautifully. I wish that she would play more often but sometimes life gets in the way.

I opened this chapter by discussing adoption and I do not want to put down the concept of adoption or the process in any way. In life, people have to do what works for them. My wife and I were able to conceive children and God was gracious enough to bless us with a boy and a girl. Both are wonderful additions to our family. I told my wife that the best days of my life were when she and I walked down the isle of St. Christopher's R.C. Church and when Marisa and Joseph were born. Diane concurs and we are very happy together and we have built a beautiful life for our family. I wouldn't change a thing, even if I could.

Robert Paster lived several blocks from my childhood home in Whitestone, Queens. The Paster's adopted a boy and a girl and tried to give their children a better life. Robert was older than I was and I don't even know what school he attended and even if he went to school. He was a big guy who worked out and was a scary dude. Everyone in the neighborhood knew of him and many people actually feared him. They had good reason to fear this person because his entire existence was based on fear and intimidation. He was a train wreck in motion and I will explain why he was the type of bully that people really should be scared of.

I had a lawn business in the neighborhood and one of my customers lived across the street from our house. Mrs. Tuerk lived on an odd-shaped block that had one row of houses on it. The front of her house was on 14th Avenue and the back of her house was on 13th Avenue. One night, she was looking at her car parked on 13th Avenue and she noticed a man climbing out of a window of one of the homes across the street. As the man climbed off the roof of this home, she noticed that he had a stereo in his arms. She immediately called the police who arrived very quickly. They caught Robert Paster red-handed as he entered his home with a stolen stereo system. He was arrested on the spot.

Mrs. Tuerk did her civic duty and she and I discussed the arrest of Robert

Paster. She was fearful of him because of his reputation. When she called the police, she did not know that he was the thief. Perhaps if she had, she might have looked the other way. After his arrest, he kept walking past her home. One day, he told her that she would pay for what she had done to him. One night after he had made these threats, there was an explosion. She didn't know what made all of that noise but she called the police to investigate. The police discovered that someone put something on Mrs. Tuerk's car that exploded and blew out the windows. The interior of her car also caught fire. Believe it or not, the car was repairable. Robert Paster continued to walk past her house to taunt her and he gave her other threatening messages but no one was ever held accountable for this crime.

Steve Barclay was one of Robert Paster's friends and he told me that Robert had been bragging about what he had done to Mrs. Tuerk. I asked this older guy how Robert had blown out all of the windows of this woman's car. He pulled out an M-80 and put it on the windshield wiper of a car. He indicated that if you put four of them together, this is equal to half of a stick of dynamite. The most important thing to consider is that you need to connect them in such a way that there is only one fuse and they all explode at the same time. I always bought one gross of M-80's (144 M-80's) every summer as did many of my friends. We used to buy them from a guy in the neighborhood for about forty bucks. I would hide them in our shed. My friends and I used to go through the neighborhood blowing things up. Most of the time, we would put one in someone's metal garbage pail. The blast would send the metal cover straight into the air. I kept this information about Robert Paster to myself. If Mrs. Tuerk ever found out, she would have told the police and then I would have been in the cross-hairs of this dangerous bully.

One of my earliest encounters with this bully took place years earlier when I was about eight years old. I was throwing a baseball with Teddy Perulo in front of my house. My house was about three blocks from the waterfront that overlooked the Throgs Neck Bridge. My friends and I always played baseball but if one of us overthrew the ball it could roll all the way to the waterfront. It was a pain in the ass to retrieve the ball, but we were young and very energetic.

Robert Paster was also very energetic. He was in great shape and really fast and agile for someone his size. He happened to walk by when Teddy and I were playing baseball. He said to me, "Joe, let me see the ball." I threw it over to him and he hurled it as far as he could. He laughed as he walked away. This baseball rolled all the way to the waterfront where the really expensive homes were. Teddy and I walked three blocks to retrieve the ball. We continued our toss in front of my house and Robert Paster returned. Again he said, "Joe let me see the ball."

I said, "sure" and ran towards him. Then I tossed the ball over his head and ran away. Teddy caught the ball and he ran down the block. Teddy and I were running and tossing the ball to each other. Robert was hot on our heels. I was very surprised about how fast he was but he caught up to me and threw me into a rose bush. Before I fell, I tossed the ball to Teddy. He then grabbed Teddy and knocked him down but not before Teddy tossed the ball back to me. All the while, we were tormenting Robert with the phrase, "Paster, Paster, you gotta run faster." After a half hour of sweating and running around, Robert gave up and left the area. Teddy and I were tired and dirty but proud of our achievement. Then we went into our pool and cooled off.

Robert Paster never really disliked me. I would never cross the guy because he would have reduced me to a bloody pulp. I knew a lot of his friends and they were all about five years older than I was. They used to hang out in front of Whitestone Drugs and I would pass by on my way home from Teddy's house. I would hang around with these guys once in a while. Teddy didn't think that this was such a good idea and he was right. These guys were bad news.

The owner of Whitestone Drugs was a man named Stu. He would tell all of the kids that hung out in front of his store to leave because he thought that it was bad for business. No one would listen. When I was fifteen years old, Steve Barclay asked me to do a favor for him. Steve knocked up his girlfriend and she wouldn't get an abortion. He didn't want anything to do with this situation. He was working in the drug store and he needed diapers but wasn't willing to pay for them. It was wintertime and I was wearing a peacoat at the time. He distracted the owner who was preparing customers prescriptions and I walked through the store and grabbed disposable diapers and put them under my coat. I stole about six packages and only stopped when there were no other diapers in the store. I stashed them under Steve's car. Later that night, he and I went to deliver the diapers. Steve made me wait in the car while he broke up with his pregnant girlfriend. When he was finished, he drove me home.

Another time, Steve gave me a lot of whiskey and then told me to steal Stu's toupee off his head. I didn't want to do it because I knew that it was wrong but he kept pumping the booze into me. I finally agreed because I didn't want to get a bad reputation with these guys. I went downstairs to the outside of the front door to enter the drug store. Stu came over to tell me to get lost. Steve was outside of the building and started kicking something. When Stu looked up, I made my move. I grabbed this greasy toupee off this man's head and ran away. It took me about five minutes to sprint home. As I entered our home, I heard police sirens. Apparently, Stu's wife told the police that an armed robbery was taking place. There was a manhunt on for Joe D'Marco who was armed (with a toupee) and dangerous. I didn't know what to do with myself, so I called my high school girlfriend. Nicole could hear the sirens. I felt like such a bad ass. Because of these antics, I had to travel a different way when going to and from Teddy's house. I had to avoid the area but I would bump into Paster and his friends in the neighborhood. When I saw Steve, I asked him what I should do with this greasy hairpiece with hair clips attached. He had Paster negotiate a deal for me. Stu didn't know my last name or where I lived. Somebody that worked in that store did know where I lived and was going to tell Stu. If my father would have found out, he really would have killed me. I gave the toupee to Paster and he returned it to Stu and received a ten-dollar reward. Then, I was told to go and apologize to Stu. I did just that and Stu wanted his ten dollars back. Then a police officer showed up and took down my information. The resulting agreement was that no one would press charges unless I continued to hang out with those kids. I forked over the re-ward money and never went back to Whitestone Drugs again.

The worst thing that Robert Paster ever did to me was to body slam me onto the hood of a car parked by the drug store. He enjoyed hurting people but that experience was not painful. When I got off the hood of the car, the hood was really crushed. I bolted out of the area because I didn't want to pay for the damage. Eventually, the guys that hung out in the area grew up and moved on with their lives. Steve Barclay eventually hurt someone so badly that he wound up in prison. Then he stabbed another prisoner and he did hard time. I never saw him again.

I never saw Robert Paster again, but he had some reputation. I heard that he opened a karate studio where he taught karate. Then he killed someone. One night on Francis Lewis Boulevard, a guy was using a pay phone. Robert Paster showed up because he wanted to use that phone. Words were exchanged and Robert Paster used a gun to kill the guy on the phone and shoot someone else who happened to be at the scene. Robert Paster was now a murderer on the run. He hid at an apartment in Florida that belonged to one of my neighbors. Matty was my age and lived two houses away from our house on 14th Avenue. When Matty's father found out that his Florida apartment was being used to harbor a felon, he contacted the police and Robert Paster was apprehended. The world is a better place with this violent bully in jail and separated from the general public. I wouldn't want to be in the same prison with this psychopath because he is truly a lethal weapon. If I sell a gun to a known terrorist, the results would be predictable. That gun would be used to hurt someone. Robert Paster was just like the terrorist. You knew that someday someone would push his buttons. That young man who died at the hands of this bully made a mistake. The decedent crossed paths with the wrong person and he paid the ultimate price. I find it very sad that this young man was never able to raise a family or enjoy life because Robert Paster was a disaster waiting for the opportunity to inflict bodily harm. On this particular night, Robert Paster crossed the line and went too far. As a result, two lives were lost and a third life was nearly destroyed. Life has consequences and this story exemplifies that point.

Bullying in the Workplace

I thought that when I was twenty-three years old I knew all that I needed to know about the world. I had recently graduated from St. John's University and was working for a major insurance carrier. My family had recently shed the shackles that we called Pat. Life was certainly more relaxed without that bully anywhere near us. I had witnessed bullying in school, been a victim of bullying at home, and had seen all sorts of situations that involved bullies in action. I never expected to see it at work. When I did see it, I was not willing to sit by idly and witness it again.

In 1990, I was a suit unit negotiator for this large automobile insurance carrier. We had extensive inventories and our cases were either going to be settled, resolved by filing motions, or were going to trial. It is interesting to note that our files were all paper and we had one computer in the office. That one computer had a green screen and could only tell us if an insured had a policy and what type of coverage the insured had.

I sat next to this attorney named James. I never liked him because I thought that he was a cocky asshole. His life was certainly not a picture of perfection. If it had been, he would have been practicing law. He was about ten years older than I was and he was getting a divorce from his wife. He actually told me that when he got married, he had a dog that had been his companion for years before he even met his wife. During the divorce, his wife insisted on getting the dog in the settlement. He asked her why she wanted the dog and her reply was, "because it is yours."

Sean was a young man who worked in the mail and file area of this office. This young man was about two to three years younger than I was and you could tell that he had some mental deficiencies. I met his father who was just happy that his son had a job and was working in a company that would protect this young man. Sean was a good kid and would never hurt anybody. Every day, Sean would come by with stacks of files and mail that was attached to these files. We would have to go through the mail and process the files. Afterwards, Sean would come by and pick up files that we had finished working and he would put the files back on the shelves. He was very responsive to all of our needs. He was always pleasant and accommodating whenever I needed help in any way. I would chat with Sean and sometimes tease him. He would tell me about his girlfriend and he would chat with the people who had desks near mine. Like I said before, this kid was harmless. James saw someone who he could ridicule and bully. Some of the things that he did and said to Sean were downright nasty. It appeared to me that James's displaced aggression due to his dysfunctional home life was being thrust upon this young mail and file employee. This went on for some time and I could tell that Sean was being affected by what James was doing to him.

Then one day, I blasted James after he said something really hurtful to Sean. I put James in his place and I stood up for a victim of bullying but it didn't matter. Sean was fired (due to his job performance) soon after this altercation. Needless to say, James and I never spoke after this episode but he never bothered Sean again. One of my longtime friends who worked in the suit unit with us recently spoke to James. He is practicing law in Florida. I told my friend Valerie what he had done to Sean years ago and that I never liked that smug asshole.

In 2004, I was working in an office located in New Hyde Park, New York. I worked with a unit of people and we all investigated car accident cases that appeared to be fraudulent. We were investigators and I had been working in this unit for five years. I led the unit in cases resolved and committee reports every year since I arrived. My raises and bonuses were based on my results and I did very well financially.

One of my coworkers was a woman named Brenda. This woman was a bitchy individual who thought that her presence was a benefit for us all. When

I first began working with her, she and I would butt heads. It was a personality thing and I refused to back down and put up with her bullshit. I was very good at what I did and certainly confident about my abilities. My record was based on my achievements and hers was based on good work but also on ass-kissing. Whenever someone new joined the unit, Brenda took it upon herself to vet them and bully them. Like I said, she pulled the same shit with me but I pushed back hard. After my initiation and response, she didn't bother me at all. In fact, I would give it back to her even when I wasn't on her radar. One day, she was going on and on with another woman about how she would raise children when the time was right. I was forty-two years old at the time and I had two children and this woman was a little younger with no children. Finally, I got annoyed with her and I said, "Yeah, yeah, yeah, and when you do have a kid, it's diapers won't stink."

Her response was short and succinct when she said, "point well taken." She then shut her pie hole and I didn't hear a peep out of her for the rest of the day.

Brad joined the unit and he needed to learn our procedures and how to do this job. I liked him and he was certainly a qualified and intelligent addition to our unit. Brenda then started her bullying with him. I heard little remarks and comments that she made to him. She bossed him around and then I heard her saying things about his weight. I didn't think that this was cool so I told her to leave him alone. She had a mind of her own and wouldn't leave him alone. Again, I told her to leave him alone. I was then transferred to another job in the same building. For the next five years, I spent my time testifying in court and at arbitration hearings. I was rarely in the office during that period of time. I would see Brad in passing and he said that he was doing well. I never had any other contact with Brenda and that wasn't such a bad thing since I was never a fan of hers.

In 2011, I was again working with Brad. I would chat with Brad all the time and one day he told me that Brenda moved away to Massachusetts and no longer worked for the company. He wasn't complaining that she was gone because she put him through hell. One day, her name came up with some other people in the office and I learned that she had given birth to a little girl. At the age of five, it was discovered that this child had leukemia. I learned of a website in her name with photos and the site shared details of this little girl's ordeal. I felt badly for the child but I couldn't help thinking about karma and Brenda was surrounded by bad karma when I knew her. I looked up the website and I felt badly when I learned about this child. This girl was told that she would feel better if she received a bone marrow transplant so she went through this additional procedure and the results were the same as before. I remember reading that when the little girl learned that the treatment had no effect on her disease, she was beside herself. I told Brad about this little girl and I gave him the information. He looked on the website and he actually made donations in that little girl's name despite how her mother had treated him. Shortly thereafter this little girl succumbed to her illness.

I left the company in 2012 and lost touch with many of the people who I worked with. One of my friends recently told me that Brad and his wife moved to Florida. This is where his parents resided. He always had a passion for boating and fishing and the weather in Florida would allow him to fish whenever he wanted. I hope that he is doing well. When I look back at his situation, I find Brad to be a really compassionate individual and a man of great character. He is also a survivor because he put up with this woman's bullying and he didn't let it affect him in a negative way.

The Most Dangerous Person in the World - The Serial Bully

I have spent most of my professional years working in the private sector and if I would have had a choice, that would have been my only work experience. When I was laid off from a position that I had held for more than a quarter of a century, I decided to try something different. I was hired for a job in the public sector as an auditor in a governmental agency. As I reflect back on my working years, I can clearly see the difference between a business that relies on revenue and profits to fund its operations and one that receives public funds to operate. There is no question that government waste runs rampant in the public sector and management is not accountable for that waste.

At the age of fifty, I was hired into this public agency. My direct supervisor was Sybil Shapiro and she was a psycho bitch. We both worked for Tom Chao who was a very nice man but his thick accent made it impossible for me to understand any conversations that I had with him. I had always thought that I was good at understanding people from other cultures since I grew up in an Italian family with many relatives having thick Italian accents. I was extremely good at imitating those family members and my sisters and I would chuckle as I went off on rants. I got the most mileage out of, "If I maka the bread, I no maka the cake. If I maka the cake, I no maka the bread." That is the excuse that was given to me when I went to a bakery to pick up a pre-ordered cake that made me two hours late for a party. I understood Mario and didn't hold it against him but my girlfriend at the time did. That is one of the reasons why she was history shortly thereafter. Spending the rest of my life with a woman that bitchy would be like spending an eternity in hell.

On my first day at work in the public sector, I met a lot of people. When I first met Sybil, I thought that she was very friendly. I also thought that she was too nice (dripping with honey) and that made me feel very uneasy. I thought that there was more there than meets the eye. She had a wedding ring on that day and then the ring was not on her finger after that first meeting. She helped me to get set up and I had to fill out forms and more forms. We had meetings and more meetings and then I had to get fingerprinted. The following week, Sybil and I sat down and really got into my new inventory. I had worked one on one with colleagues in the past but this woman was so overbearing that I could not breathe. Through it all, I felt that she was flirting with me. I tried to not pay attention to her flinging her hair back constantly and I found her outfits very revealing. My way of dealing with this woman was to talk about my wife and kids. She probably got annoyed when I mentioned that my wife was an RN and I did mention that fact over and over again. I also had family photos on my desk. Sybil and I were together frequently at my desk in the beginning of my time at this new position. It took me less than a week to size up Sybil. She was married to a businessman and they had one child. Her marriage was in a state of flux during my tenure at this job. I recently learned that she is now officially divorced. Years ago, she had an affair with Stan on the third floor who I used to chat with. He was also married. I have known many women in my lifetime who came from homes where they did not get enough attention from their fathers. Those daddy issues made them look for attention in their relationships. In a lot of those cases, they couldn't get enough attention and they were wacky. Sybil's parents were divorced and she had step brothers and extended family members. From what she told me, her family was not so different from many other American families. Sybil's husband did eventually run away and I am certain that he felt Sybil's wrath, as I did for the two years that I worked for her. The Sybil that I knew was a total bitch, narcissist, and an alcoholic.

My desk was located in a tiny cubicle and Sybil would pull her chair in behind mine. She would constantly lean over my shoulder and point out things on my computer screen. If I pushed the wrong key, she would be on me in a second. She was just too overbearing for my taste. Poor Stan had an affair with her and he was such a nice guy. Sybil was so bossy that I can just imagine her bossing him around in the bedroom. "Stan, a little higher and to the left. That's not it, I said to the left." I hope Stan moved on, but if not she's a keeper!

Sybil and I got off to a rocky start because I was not some kid who just graduated from college and working for this agency was my dream come true. After working in close quarters with this woman for one week, I asked her if I could work on my own and if I had any questions, I would come to her for advice. She seemed put off, but agreed. We proceeded like this for the next year. I was reviewed by management at quarterly intervals. After every review, I was told that everything was great with no complaints. I told my wife that for what they were paying me, the government was getting a steal.

During my first year, I did notice that Sybil was too controlling. As I talked to people in the office, I learned that Sybil had had problems with Rhonda who sat at a desk across from my desk. Rhonda was very nice and worked for a different supervisor. I was chatting with Rhonda one day and then Sybil called me into a conference room. I was told that I was not to speak with Rhonda at all. She wouldn't tell me why but I told her that I would heed her advice. I went home and told my wife that no one has ever told me that I couldn't speak with someone. I felt like I was in high school. Here we were in a business atmosphere and I was forbidden to speak with a coworker. Then I was told that I shouldn't be speaking to other coworkers and I couldn't use the shredder during business hours. At that point, I felt like I just woke up in Nazi Germany. My defense to Sybil was that my work was getting done but I would do as she asked. I was wondering if she was going to revoke my bathroom privileges next! I told my coworkers that things were not like this in the private sector and I would have to get used to this kind of scrutiny and control.

After that first year working for this agency, my health began to fail. I looked healthy but you cannot judge a book by its cover. My manager would complain that I did not do this or did not do that. I would apologize and would fix the issue that she had. Sybil got on my case more and more frequently as time went on and her tone became more and more bitchy. All the while, I just dealt with it and kept my mouth shut and continued to be respectful.

My wife describes me and my son as two individuals who get pushed and pushed and then when it is time to push back, we shove back. People watch this play out and then can't believe their eyes. When my son was two years-old he was playing with his cousin Michael. Michael was one year older and the boys were playing nicely. My wife saw Michael poking Joseph in the chest repeatedly. Joseph took it until it was time to push back. He shoved Michael so hard that my nephew went flying into a TV set and fell down. Then he cried and my sister came to his aid. My wife stepped in at that point and explained what had happened. My sister then yelled at her son. All I can say is that the apple does not fall far from the tree and my "Mini-Me" is no different than I am.

Sybil did not know who she was dealing with when she started bullying me. Then one day, it happened. I shoved back and Tom and Sybil did not appreciate it. I was such a good employee until I put them on notice. I shoved back and Sybil could have worked it out with me. Her DNA would not allow her to work with me at all. My words were powerful and my arguments were pertinent. I did explain that I had not been feeling well which I had stated previously but no one was listening. People do not believe that someone is ill unless they see a cast or a deformity because they need that visual aid to believe. In addition, I had summoned the total bitch in Sybil after working for her for one and a half years. It was a boundary that we both crossed due to circumstances beyond our control.

I have worked for people who were wet behind the ears and my experience was intimidating to them. Sybil was a supervisor for the previous seven years and worked for this agency for fifteen years. I once said to her that it probably wasn't fair to her that they placed me under her supervision since I had thirty-two years of business experience which was more than twice her tenure with this agency. She naturally responded that this had no bearing on our situation. Sybil continued to break my balls and I reciprocated in kind. Everything was a battle and then my eighteen month review was given to me. When she presented it to me, she left the conference room door open because she was scared of what I might do. I objected because people were walking by and could hear us arguing. I refused to sign the document because it was setting me up for failure in addition to not being truthful. Everything that she had thrown at me, I was able to push back. Then my health issues really kicked in. I was out of work for three weeks and then returned to work against my doctor's advice. I returned to this hell hole and I battled with Sybil on a daily basis.

After my initial illness, I returned to work. It was during this time that I filed a complaint with human resources. I put them on notice that I was in a protected class due to the Americans with Disabilities Act. I also provided documentation from my treating physicians and I provided the serial number of the St. Jude device that was in the mitral valve of my heart. All of a sudden, the dynamics of my situation with this governmental agency changed dramatically. It was an "oh shit" moment for these morons. Their position up to this point was that he looks fine therefore he is full of shit. They continued to sing this song even after I had another device implanted into my chest. In my opinion, Sybil was not the only delusional person working for this agency.

I commented previously that government managers do not have to be accountable for their actions because they are funded by tax dollars. This agency sent me for three weeks of training at a considerable cost to the taxpayers. The managers never tried to work with me because their only focus was to get rid of me after I put up a fight. They never exhibited any compassion or empathy and treated me horribly. In the past four years since I have been retired, the turnover rate has remained very high and they cannot keep qualified people in their offices. They are the most incompetent and inept people that I have ever met. Years later, some of those management people have been replaced but the office is still a hell hole and the turnover rate continues to remain high. The office morale remains very low and they just can't keep their offices staffed properly. They use short-sighted approaches to run the offices and their thinking was never out of the box. The government mantra has always been to maintain the status quo. There is and never will be rewards for innovative ideas.

A serial bully has no empathy and they enjoy witnessing the results of their attacks on their targets. They basically manipulate their targets and the people around the office and as a result they control the narrative. I witnessed this first hand as Sybil's actions took place behind closed doors so people could not see what was happening. When I pushed back, she brought in Tom. I have seen her messages to Tom and a review of those documents indicates that she manipulated his perception of the situation. Together they plotted the end game for my future in this agency. During the second year of my employment, Sybil continued with her phony facade. She and I would argue and she would leave the conference room with a big smile and ask people what they were doing next weekend. She takes the cake when it comes to phony bitches!

In researching this serial bullying issue, I noted that the targets are usually people who are very competent and very good at their jobs. In a lot of cases, they are people who have never been on the receiving end of any disciplinary actions in their entire careers. This was my story as well. When my issues with Sybil started to heat up, I had thirty-two years of business experience with an unblemished career. The only issues that I had previously were health issues and my former employers understood my heart issues and worked with me over the years. I worked twenty-seven years for my previous employer and during my tenure there, I missed about twelve months of work due to surgeries, hospitalizations, and recoveries. I always felt that my health history kept my career from advancing but that did not hinder my ability to provide them with great results year after year. Had my heart condition ended my career while in the private sector, I believe that they would have taken good care of me and my transition into retirement would have been seamless.

This could not be the story while working for the government because of the people involved and especially because of their collective incompetence. When I was initially hired in this position, I did not tell anyone about my health situation. I was afraid that it would be used against me. I was especially careful around Sybil. She did what most serial bullies do, she tried to become my buddy. As nice as she was to me in the beginning, I was careful about what information I offered. Many serial bullies try to befriend their targets and then they stab their targets in the back and use it against them. In this case, I did not provide much information that could be used in this manner. I did not keep this information to myself for any other reason other than this was personal information that I chose not to share. Like I said earlier, I was onto this woman from day one. I tend to be cautious with people who are always dripping with honey. I like honey but only in my tea!

Targets of bullying sometimes refer to themselves as victims. I do not consider myself a victim or someone who needed pity. I am a very competent individual with great credentials. Those credentials were so impressive that I was hired out of a pool of two hundred applicants with several other coworkers. Targets sometimes breakdown and cry in front of the bully and this just fuels the bully's efforts further. I noted in my research that usually within two years of becoming a target, the target is no longer working at that job. Many of the outcomes lead to resignations, terminations, illnesses, and suicides. In the instant case, the government wanted to terminate me, but I became gravely ill and held onto my position until I was ready to resign. That burned them up and Sybil was especially pissed off because my replacement could not use my desk until I resigned. She was forced to walk into another portion of the office to confer with her other employees. My coworkers referred to my desk area as "The Shrine."

I have always been a confident person who tends to be intimidating. The intimidating part is not by design but it makes me laugh when people describe me in this fashion. When family members say something stupid, I respond without any hesitation to shut them down. I show them the ridiculousness of their statements with facts that destroy their comments. This can be intimidating if your bullshit views go unchallenged by the simpletons who buy into that stuff hook, line, and sinker.

Sybil would make ridiculous statements and assertions and I would fire back immediately. One day she stated something that really pissed me off. She said, "your work product looks like you don't care."

My response was sudden and swift when I stated, "I am personally insulted and no one has ever said that to me and I have been in the business world for thirty-two years." This type of push-back challenges the bully and in the instant case, she stuttered and had no response. This type of back and forth became the norm with our relationship. You could cut the tension with a knife and other people did notice. I was asked by coworkers about what was going on and I replied that I could not discuss anything as I did not want to be part of the soap opera culture that existed in the office.

Having the facts to respond to such bullying is very important. I was constantly correcting my supervisor during our closed-door meetings during my second year and she would respond by saying to me, "How do you remember this stuff?" Many times, I would give her a little advice and then she started writing down my comments. When I knew that the management was looking at termination in my case, I asked a question of her that she did not expect. I said to her, "If my work product does not improve within the next six months, what will happen?" She said that I would be terminated. This threat on her part was emphatically denied by their counsel when I filed an EEOC Complaint with the federal government.

It was obvious to me that she was out of her depth and I told her so. I didn't break down and cry but rather I would push back so forcibly that she would keep the door open for fear of physical harm. Granted I was taller than she was and probably outweighed her by eighty pounds but I was capable of destroying her with my words and I knew that.

One day I told her that life was like a chess game. She needed elaboration on that statement so I continued by stating that I would counter her moves with my own. She needed to write down my comments verbatim but my message was simple. I was not going to go down without a fight and I eventually proved that to be true. All the while, I remembered what a colleague told me years earlier. Rosemary Posto told me in 1985, "you can't fight city hall but you can shit on the steps." As funny as this statement is, it is so very true. These morons in upper management made a big mistake in trusting a woman who was a psychopathic liar. They relied on her evaluation of our situation. The problem was that Sybil needed to lie to cover her misdeeds, mental instability, alcoholism, and her prior history. In addition, her attitude of being a know-it-all did not serve her well. Her medical opinion of me was very important to the management team. I said to my coworkers that her medical expertise was sorely missed when Dr. Taylor performed life-saving surgeries on me years earlier. I stated that he could have used her input during the operations. I was being facetious as Dr. Taylor performed open-heart procedures on many patients at St. Francis Hospital and his specialty was operating on infants. His golden hands saved my life when I was thirty-five years old and obviously God had a plan for me. Perhaps Gods' plan included my son who was born nearly two years after that surgery.

The management in this office never once spoke to me to see what was really going on. Their management style was absent which leads right back to my prior comments about their incompetence. Years later, they have all been replaced. One of my coworkers actually said to me that "no one has ever pushed these people back and they deserve to be put in their places. You will be the one to change all of that." I wish that this was true but their lives continued and mine went from sixty miles per hour to about ten miles per hour. I know from my years in business that once someone is tapped on the shoulder to get into management, the managers will need a tsunami to throw that person under the bus. It was obvious to me that Sybil was in good standing with her superiors. I actually told my coworkers to avoid talking to me since I was so toxic.

I contacted human resources to file a complaint with their department. I sent a letter with the requisite language for the Americans with Disabilities Act and then supplemented it with letters from two different physicians. There was no doubt that I was entitled to protection under that law. Then I asked for a transfer to another supervisor, one without an axe to grind. It took nine months for them to respond to that letter. Michelle Tinsdale only responded when she was told that I had additional heart surgery. This turned out to be another "oh shit" moment. At first, I thought that this woman would actually try to help me. In the end, she dropped the ball so badly that she wound up having to retire. Her incompetence was evident to me and my understanding was that she had a reputation for not doing her job. Not only was she at the top of the pay scale, but she was a director of an entire department. Again, we are talking about government managers so this should not be a big surprise.

I also contacted my union representative since I was being forced to pay union dues. I laid out my case to Serena Smalls and when I disagreed with her plan of attack, she refused to take my calls. She also turned out to be a *waste of vital organs*. She did inform me that Sybil had a history with the union since many complaints had been filed against this unhinged supervisor. She called Sybil a "total bitch," which only confirmed my opinion of my supervisor.

Joanna Casey worked several cubicles away from my desk. She was a representative for the union who also worked as an auditor. I had always chatted with her in the office. I asked to speak with her outside of the office. I didn't know where else to turn. She was the angel that came to my rescue. She and I would take coffee breaks and discuss my health issues and how they affected my job performance. She also had significant health issues that she had to deal with. Joanna was able to help me to deal with this nut job who was making me ill. Conversations with Joanna were very enlightening and made me realize that I was not alone in my feelings of disgust for this wacky supervisor who had the power to destroy people's lives. If I would have died prior to filing my complaint, Sybil would have shown up at my wake. She would have extended her condolences to my wife and kids knowing full well that she put me in an early grave.

Joanna told me that Sybil always had a problem with the people that worked for her. Rhonda had consulted with Joanna about her issues when she worked for Sybil. Sybil had destroyed her but when I saw Rhonda's work product, I understood why. Rhonda was the worst employee ever and her work product was abysmal. Since they could not fire her due to her seniority, she was bounced from one supervisor to the next. The reason that Rhonda was transferred away from Sybil was because she filed a discrimination complaint that was handled by the same executive in human resources who I had contacted. Joanna did not reveal this information to me. I was able to piece all of this together by speaking with my coworkers and it all made sense.

I had the opportunity to work with Jesse Benjamin. He is an individual who worked at this agency for thirteen years in a different department. He was very competent and had done very well for the agency over the years. He was moved over to our unit and began working for Sybil. She was nice to him and then she began to break his balls. She continued to bully this man until he couldn't take it anymore. He was able to pull some strings and get transferred to another supervisor. He was one of the lucky ones since he survived his ordeal.

When I was working, there was a woman named Diana who sat in the next cubicle. She was a good worker and always helped me out when I asked. She and I got along famously. We both worked for Sybil and she worked for Sybil for many years. Sybil made Diana's life miserable when she first started working at this agency. After Diana completed her probation, things improved significantly. As the years went on, Diana kept producing with excellent results. She certainly earned her salary. All the while, I could see that she was petrified of Sybil. Now that Sybil had destroyed all other potential targets, she was focusing on Diana and I felt terrible for this lovely and competent woman.

My research indicates that serial bullies destroy one target and usually move onto another target within two weeks. I was not at this job for a long enough period to gauge how accurate this information is. What I can say is that the documentation that I reviewed is on the money if you take a look at this one small agency. Sybil began to fine tune her tortuous actions with Rhonda and started bullying her until she filed a complaint and was moved to another unit. Then Joe D'Marco came along and in my second year, it became unbearable and I nearly lost my life. I got out due to health reasons at age fifty-two. After I was out of the picture, she bullied Jesse Benjamin for a long period of time until he got switched to another supervisor. Then she focused on Diana who is vested in the pension plan and I suspect will retire and get out of Dodge in the near future. Sybil then shifted gears and was working on the destruction of a woman who has worked for the department for at least ten years. Most of these people, including myself, were competent individuals. There is no question that Sybil is a serial bully and she is dangerous.

A friend recently told me that Sybil is still a supervisor but she does not have any subordinates. This type of change is probably the best possible move since she does not get along with anyone. In the private sector, she would have been fired. At this point, no one has died from her bullying, but I certainly came close.

When my health started to decline in 2014, I was treated by several doctors. My initial instinct was to reach out to my cardiologist since my heart history had been a factor in my life since I was five years old. The tests came back normal but I really did not feel well. It took an additional year for the electrical problems in my heart to reach critical mass and put me in a situation where I was told that I could suffer a massive heart attack. It was at that time that I needed a defibrillator/pace maker to keep me alive. I would go to my doctors and they would treat symptoms but we never found out what the root of the problem was until income tax day in 2015. I thought that I was suffering from chronic fatigue syndrome because I had the symptoms for this ailment, but in the end it was far more serious.

Targets such as myself in bullying cases have noted some or all of the following symptoms:

- anger and confusion about what had happened
- sleep deprivation
- constant fatigue
- palpitations and panic attacks
- cognitive dysfunction
- lack of concentration and other physical limitations

Many of these symptoms are not exhibited by the targets externally and the bully can say that there is nothing wrong with the target. This is apparently what happened in my case and it fits Sybil's narrative. People see me now and say that I look great but my chest looks like something out of a *Rambo movie*. I have scars from three open heart procedures and a large hole and depression where a chest tube once resided. In addition, you can see the bulge from the ICD (Implantable Cardioverter Defibrillator) which is about the size of a pack of cigarettes. My heart only operates at 40% and if it gets much worse I will need a heart transplant. The brain surgeons working at that governmental agency probably still think that I am full of shit. The government actually sent in-house investigators to conduct surveillance on me. Perhaps they thought that they would catch me running a marathon or something! One day when my wife was taking me to physical therapy, she stopped to confront one of these idiots. He stuttered so badly that we couldn't understand him. They kept checking on me periodically and I was able to watch them using my whole house video surveillance system. They reminded me of John Candy in his role as a bumbling private investigator in the movie *Who's Harry Crumb?*

Twenty-five years ago, I had a heart episode during a stress test that scared the shit out of the doctors at St. Francis Hospital. The electrical system in my heart went crazy when they got my heart rate up to two hundred beats per minute. I was a young man at the time and not your typical heart patient. While in the hospital for all of my procedures over the years, I was usually the youngest patient on the floor. Since I exhibited electrical problems prior to my open-heart procedures, it makes sense that sooner or later I would have needed to be treated by an electrophysiologist. The stress that any job causes probably would have been enough to put me into a tail spin. When you factor in the negative stress caused by a serial bully, the odds of this happening multiply exponentially. I faced many of the challenges that most targets experience including:

- the loss of my career and job
- major health issues
- noticeable lifestyle changes
- the possibility of losing our home
- the possible destruction of our family life
- the potential loss of my marriage

When it was apparent that my career was over and I could no longer work, I sat down with my mother. I explained my situation and her words still echo in my ears today. She said, "I am surprised you lasted this long." She knew that I have been battling heart issues since I was a child so this was not a shock for her. She took care of my health issues and dealt with them because my father had no interest in dealing with a sick child. I don't think that he could ever deal with the emotional trauma of dealing with a sick loved one. His way of dealing with a sick child was to delegate it to someone else. He was never sick in his entire life and he lacked empathy just like many of the bullies who are out there making people's lives miserable. Why do they do it? **Because they can.**

It also took a while for the rest of my family to get used to the idea that I could no longer work. I have to say that all of our family members were okay with the idea. It was certainly a life-changing event for us. I agree with my wife that given my medical history, this end result should not have been totally unexpected. We both feel that Sybil exacerbated my health issues to a point where I had to stop working and stop being a productive member of society.

My wife, Diane, really stepped up to the plate. Once she got used to the idea of her husband being home 24/7, she was okay with the situation. Being a registered nurse was really a blessing for me. She has been there every step of the way. In addition to being the most compassionate person that I know, she is a great cook. I guess that I can blame her for the extra twenty pounds that I have gained since being home! She monitors my salt intake, my many medications, and everything else that comes with taking care of a disabled individual.

Just for the record, she knew about my heart history when we first met and she was okay with my issues. Diane came to my softball games in the late 1980s and saw me hitting home runs and running the bases. She might have thought to herself, *What heart problem?* My description of my life at this time continues to be that I was cruising along at sixty mph and then I hit a wall. I have no choice but to live my life now at ten mph. The wall that I hit has a name and it was called Sybil Shapiro.

After I resigned my position, my personal belongings were mailed to me. A special photo and beautiful frame that my daughter had given to me was in the box but it was smashed to pieces. The photo was a picture of me and my little girl dancing at her "Sweet Sixteen" party. I know that Sybil would have been the person who emptied my desk and packed my belongings into the box. I can just picture what went on that day, as she smashed the frame and said, "Oops, that's such a shame." I am okay with it because replacing a picture frame is easier than replacing a person's life.

Conclusion

When you read this book cover to cover, you might wonder why I spent years writing this book. To me, the answer is very simple. I had a story to tell. It was a personal story which I needed to convey in a straightforward and honest way. Some of the names in this book have been changed because we live in a very litigious society. I wanted to get my story out but I did not want to spend my remaining days on earth defending lawsuits. **What I have written here is the truth**.

My kids don't believe that I have a good sense of humor. Diane has always laughed at my jokes and it is not because she has to. There have been things that I have said and done over the years that have made her almost pee in her pants. It's healthy to enjoy your spouse and enjoy your time together. Diane and I have that. We have a great marriage and no one on earth knows me better than my wife of twenty-six years and counting. My sister Donna recently said that we "are a hoot" and I can't disagree with her at all.

A young couple lives in the house next door to us for the last two years. The previous owners were Matt and Lisa Holly. Years ago, Lisa was yelling at her husband and I really felt badly for the public abuse that Matt was suffering through. He turned to my wife and said, "Why do I put up with this shit?" It was obvious that he was emasculated and his wife wore the pants in the family. Joe is the new owner and yesterday he was putting his Christmas decorations on his house. These decorations included a dozen of these big colorful balls which Lisa left for the new owners. When Diane came home last night, I said to her, "I found Matt's balls, they're hanging on that tree over there." We both laughed and went into our home.

Jay Berger always told me that I have a lot of really good stories. He still cannot get over the fact that I remember things that were said to us in grade school. Writing this book was a way to showcase my storytelling abilities. I was also able to inject humor into my stories. It is important to note that my observations are heartfelt. I have had a lifetime to analyze why things occurred in my life and why certain people treated me the way that they did. My purpose was never to harp on the past, it was just to explain why my life took the direction that it did.

There is one thing that never did escape me and that is that **Pat is a bully and will always be a bully.** He is not much different than other bullies who I have met in my lifetime. They all have similar character traits, they destroy people and never empathize about the way they are treating their targets. If they were empathetic people, they would never engage in such destructive behavior.

I don't believe that bullies care about what they are doing to their victims. When the bullies destroy their victims, they need to search for a new target to destroy. This lack of empathy is prevalent amongst bullies. A lack of empathy is also prevalent amongst pedophiles. Let's be clear, my story has nothing to do with sexual misconduct. I am merely drawing a correlation between what bullies and pedophiles have in common. The common thread is destructive behavior that severely compromises their victims. The pedophiles do not care what happens to their victims. They use and abuse their victims and when they are done, they discard them like yesterday's trash.

Afterwards, the victims of bullies are left to pick up the pieces. Professional help is needed to help the victims to get their lives together. Sometimes victims cannot afford to get help. Other times, they are not willing to relive their harrowing ordeals. If the targets cannot deal with what has been done to them, the end result might not be very good. What is done to people at the hands of bullies can last a lifetime. It can be detrimental to the target's ability to live a normal life. I have lived a good life and Pat's abusive behavior towards me when I was young is all in the past.

When I told my family members that I was writing this book, the only people who supported me were my wife and my kids. Everyone else thought that it was a bad idea. They expressed feelings that I shouldn't dwell on the past. They thought that it might be bad for my psyche. I assured them that I am a positive person and I don't dwell on the past.

Now my project is completed and I feel great about this accomplishment. It has not set me back. To me, it is evident that this book has propelled me forward. This entire process has initiated a new chapter in my life because Pat resides in my older chapters. He is and will always be in the past. Like I said to him in my letter, "life does go on." I will be clinging to my family as I get older and I will be in good company. Pat will have a few relatives to see on the holidays and he can cling to his scotch. He has four grandchildren and one great grandchild and he will miss them grow up and start families. He will miss the joys of new life and new unions but life has choices and there are consequences to those choices. I wish him the best and I do pray for him. I wouldn't trade places with him for all of the money in the world.

One of the benefits of writing this book was to highlight how I differ from my father the bully. I realize now that I have overcome his attempts to diminish me. It is similar to writing a list of pros and cons. In this case, my lists highlight how Pat has done things and how I have handled the same types of situations. It also exemplifies how I have learned from Pat's mistakes and made the necessary corrections so as to not follow his path. My list showcases that I am a much better husband and father than he ever was. He would obviously disagree with my assessment as he wrote that I was a "sorry excuse for a man." In a democratic society, we are all entitled to our opinions and I am okay with his parting shot. My nuclear family disagrees with his assessment and they will never abandon me as Pat's family has done. That is simply because I am a good person and he is not.

The purpose of writing this book was never to make money. The purpose was to tell the story of my life and how I was subjected to bullying by one person in particular. It concentrates on how his actions affected me and affected the people around him. It also explains why I have such hatred for Pat. He claims that he could see the hatred in my eyes. I will admit that I was never a good actor. I knew this growing up and it explains why I never moved to Hollywood! Now that my doctors have sliced my body up like a piece of filet mignon, I will never realize my dream of being an underwear model!

Whenever I went for job interviews, I would tell the interviewers that I was "articulate on paper and in person." They found out when they hired me that I was very capable of getting my point across. I had no problem speaking my mind and it worked for me. My employers benefited from my ability to communicate. This only enhanced my negotiation skills. I worked in business for thirty-two years and I always produced for my employers. I earned my salary and my raises and bonuses always reflected a job well done.

Victor was one of my supervisors in the insurance industry. He knew that I was a good communicator. In a bold move, he tapped me to lead a unit that would arbitrate cases on full time basis. This arbitration process resolved legal issues in a special forum. This unit eventually grew to four full time employees and was a very successful program. In the end, I testified on six hundred cases with an 85% success rate. I also testified on hundreds of civil and criminal fraud trials in the New York State court system. Again, I was an articulate witness and this was reflected in the results.

Based on the above, it makes sense that I could put my feelings down on paper and convey a positive message about a very difficult subject. My first beating was at the age of five, so that means that I was subjected to fear, intimidation, and bullying for about thirteen years. Thirteen years qualifies me as an expert. Pat was someone who was supposed to protect his young family, instead he preyed upon them. Pat did a number on all of us and it was as prevalent as the sun rising in the morning. The results of this constant deluge that was dumped on us on a daily basis was not evident in a visual sense. It burrowed itself under the surface and continued to play havoc with us internally. My mother's colitis flared up and she wound up in the hospital on many occasions. My sisters and I suffered with peptic ulcers which again was a result of living under Pat's roof. The pressure on us was constant. I felt like I was living in a pressure cooker that was simmering and it didn't take much for the pressure to intensify and eventually explode.

The issues that I have described only apply to the physiological issues that we endured. Many targets of bullying suffer with mental issues as well. If you think of this from a practical perspective, the mental part of the equation can be just as devastating as the physical maladies. When someone is beaten down on a daily basis, it has to surface somewhere. The targets of bullies feel worthless and that can lead to severe depression and in some cases, death.

I stated earlier that I didn't feel like a victim and wasn't looking for sympathy. That might be the way that I feel today, but I was victimized by my father on a constant basis as I lived in his house. My mother and sisters were also victimized by this man as well. When we did something that he objected to, we blamed ourselves and made excuses. When a battered wife gets a black eye from the batterer, she uses excuses like "I fell and hit the door." I have also heard victims say "it was my fault" and they were convinced by the abuser that they were at fault. Today, people see right through those excuses because we are more informed. My mother, sisters, and I lived our lives in much the same way as the battered wife. There is no question that we were victims of domestic abuse.

I recently stated to Diane that Pat has a stain on his soul and I don't. Pat has to live with what he has done. Perhaps that is why he enjoys his booze so much. Pat needs to drink to wash away his sins so he can avoid the truth. Sooner or later, he will be judged. God will not be fooled by his lies and deceit.

Our family suffered through a very difficult period of time at the hands of a bully. We were victims, there is no question about that. Today, we do not feel guilty and make excuses for Pat the bully. Other victims of bullies should not feel guilty either. These victims were not seeking out their bully and certainly weren't asking for the complications and pain that resulted from the bullying. The victims had no control over those circumstances just like we cannot control the weather. My father, just like other bullies, has to face the consequences of his actions and God's justice will be meted out.

I always described my father as a "mental midget." There is no question that he has some mental issues. I am not a psychiatrist, so I cannot diagnose his issues. I can say with certainty that Pat thinks that there is nothing wrong with his state of mind. That being said, he thinks that there is something wrong with many of the people around him. I am sure that if you spoke with

Pat about me, you would get an earful. There have been many times when I walked away shaking my head in disbelief. His views and comments can, at times, be out there.

My sister Sally threw a party at her home many years ago. Pat and Joanne had recently married. They were still in the honeymoon stage. They were talking about having a baby and how beautiful it would be. We all knew that Pat had been snipped years earlier and we didn't know if his new wife was aware of this important fact. My sisters and I huddled around and discussed how messed up any child of theirs would be. Pat was a lousy father and Joanne's son hated her and actually told us what a lousy mother she was. None of us wanted to see that couple bring any more kids into the world. It was not about money or inheritance, it was about how miserable any child of theirs would have been living with these two selfish and cold individuals. Thank God that Pat and Joanne never procreated.

So, what was the purpose of writing this book? Was it to show what a great guy I was? No, it was to illustrate that bullies come in all shapes and sizes. It was to let people know that bullies can live right next door and within the same family unit. It was to show that people who we trust, people in positions of authority, might be willing to bully their family members in order to get what they want. It illustrates the fact that weaker and younger people in our families can be victimized by their parents, grandparents, or siblings.

I had no choice but to suck it up and deal with my situation. Like the squirrels who are born in a nest forty feet above the ground, I did not know any better. I thought that all kids were beaten by their father's. I thought that all kids feared their fathers as I feared my parent. I relied on this man to guide me through life, but I realized early on that he was no role model. Even if he was capable of providing guidance to me, I wanted nothing to do with him. By the same token, my mother did the best that she could to help her children. Her time was limited since she worked full time. She was willing to intervene during Pat's fits of rage. Marie knew that she would be putting herself into the line of fire but she also knew that she had to protect her children. Marie was always a warm, compassionate, and loving person. Conversely, Pat is as cold as a dead fish. They say that opposites attract and it does apply in this situation.

If there is any lesson to be learned from this book, it is that bullying is unacceptable. We are all witnesses to some sort of bullying in our lifetimes. Hopefully, none of my readers will be the target of any bullies. We should all try to help the targets of the bullies if at all possible. I wish that I would have done more for some of the targets that I saw being picked on like Terry Murray.

I am eternally grateful to that sixth grader who got off at my bus stop to prevent one of her classmates from bullying me when I was a first grader. Her efforts helped to keep my blood in my body instead of dripping all over the sidewalk. She is the person to emulate in our fight against bullies. God bless her for helping a little kid out and for doing the right thing. She had no idea that when I went home I was subjected to a bigger and worse bully than anyone could have imagined. She had the spirit and bravery that is needed to counter bullying and I admire her for that. I wish that more people were willing to be bold enough and selfless enough to take action like she did on that sunny afternoon in Queens.

References

Introduction

Webster's New World Dictionary, Third College Edition, page 184;

**Bullying is Unacceptable –
yesterday, today and in the
future. No one deserves to
BE BULLIED...............**

One Man – 3 Helpless Victims

They were not the only ones

There were many victims over

the years.

This is the story of a monster who had a

negative impact on the lives of many

THE BULLYING CONTINUES TO THIS DAY!

About the Authors

Xavier J. D'Marco is a retired Auditor who has a Political Science Degree from St. John's University as well as an Accounting Degree from Molloy College. He spent his work career working in Insurance and Accounting.

Diane C. D'Marco is a Registered Nurse who began her career in Obstetrics and Gynecology. Today, she specializes in Pediatrics. Diane is currently licensed in 5 states.

Diane and Joe live in Long Island, New York. They have been married for nearly 27 years. They reside in their home with their two adult children and 4 dogs.

Joe thought about writing this book for years. With the urging of his wife, he began putting his thoughts down on paper. This collaboration describes the story of a man who is lucky to be alive and who is only here due to modern medicine. His extraordinary story does not focus on his health, although it does indicate the struggles affiliated with facing his own mortality. The major focus of this literary work is based on his struggles with bullies, and in particular, one bully who lived in his home. His Father bullied him from early on in life and that bullying continued through his formidable years. This book shares his story and is a testament to one man's sheer determination to follow his own path, one that did not include repeating his abusive past. It is a heartwarming story about triumph and survival that could have only taken place in this modern era.

www.ingramcontent.com/pod-product-compliance
Lightning Source LLC
Chambersburg PA
CBHW061518050726
47593CB00002B/622